WATER GARDEN
IDEA BOOK

WATER GARDEN

IDEA BOOK

LEE ANNE WHITE

The Taunton Press

For my nieces, Mary Griffin, Emma, and Jenrette

Text © 2008 by The Taunton Press, Inc.

The Taunton Press, Inc., 63 South Main Street, PO Box 5506, Newtown, CT 06470-5506
e-mail: tp@taunton.com

Editor: Carolyn Mandarano
Interior Layout: Laura Lind Design
Illustrator: Christine Erikson
Front Cover Photographers: (top row, left to right) © Lee Anne White, © Mark Turner, © Lee Anne White,
© Lee Anne White; (middle row, left to right) © Lee Anne White, © Jerry Pavia, © www.carolynbates.com,
© Allan Mandell; (bottom row, left to right) © Allan Mandell, © Dency Kane, © J. Paul Moore, © Alan
& Linda Detrick
Back Cover Photographers: (top) © Lee Anne White; (bottom, left to right) © Alan & Linda Detrick,
© Allan Mandell, © Alan & Linda Detrick

Library of Congress Cataloging-in-Publication Data
White, Lee Anne.
  Water garden idea book / Lee Anne White.
    p. cm.
  ISBN 978-1-56158-877-0
  1. Water gardens. I. Title.

SB423.W49 2008
635.9'674--dc22

                          2007016957

Printed in China
10 9 8 7 6 5 4 3 2 1

Acknowledgments

As a kid, I spent long summer afternoons at the neighborhood pond chasing bullfrogs, tadpoles, and butterflies. It was a favorite gathering place for anyone under driving age who didn't squirm at the sensation of muck between their toes or something squiggling in their hands. I'm quite sure I owe my love of garden ponds and other water features, at least in part, to those early days as an amateur naturalist.

Garden designer and contractor Mark Fockele grew up just a stone's throw from this same pond, and I wonder about its influence on him. Beautiful ponds, waterfalls, dry streams, or fountains are almost always the central attraction of any work by The Fockele Garden Company. These water features and our conversations about them were a constant source of inspiration while I worked on this book.

Others were generous in sharing their knowledge and creativity as well. Naomi Sachs of the Therapeutic Landscapes Resource Center reinforced in my mind what a powerful healing force water and gardens can be to those who are disabled, ill, or dealing with any of life's challenges. Paul Cowley, landscape architect and owner of Potomac Waterworks, along with his wife, artist Robin Cowley, opened my eyes to the true possibilities of water in the garden. I was mesmerized by the almost magical force of water in the high desert by the creative works of Clemens & Associates, Stone Forest, and sculptor Joshua Gannon. I am fortunate to live near three excellent resources for anyone interested in water gardens: Atlanta Water Gardens, Wakoola Water Gardens, and The Water Garden. And I was treated to a feast for the eyes and ears by

designers Jeff Bale, Stephen Carruthers, Dan Cleveland, Margaret de Haas van Dorsser, Michelle Derviss, Sydney Eddison, David Ellis, David Feix, Desert Sage Builders, Keith Geller, Bill Hewitt, Anna Kondolf, Little and Lewis, David McMullin, Richard McPherson, Carrie Nimmer, Rob Norris, Ben Page, Paula Refi, Michael Thilgen, Warren Simmonds, Juan Arzola, P.O.P.S. Landscaping, WaterColors, Jeni Webber, and Hermann Weis.

To the folks at The Taunton Press, thanks for your ongoing support and encouragement for more than 10 years now. It has especially been a pleasure to work with Carolyn Mandarano, who somehow manages to remain levelheaded no matter what is going on in my life, her life, or the publishing world.

And finally, my thanks and love to Alan, who quietly overlooks the dusty house, the wild garden, and the late dinners because he knows I'm happily peering through the lens of my camera into someone else's garden.

Contents

Introduction

Among my earliest and fondest childhood memories is feeding the goldfish with my grandmother in her small backyard pond on Sunday afternoons. I had never seen such large goldfish in an aquarium, and watching them swim around was probably one of the few things I would sit still for as a child. These days, I take equal pleasure in watching my nieces feed the goldfish in their grandmother's pond. And I can still sit for long periods watching the fish as they dart about the water, hiding beneath ledges or lily pads, and kissing the pond's surface for air and food. Often, it's these simple pleasures that bring us some of the greatest joys in life.

Of course, it's not just children and grownups that enjoy water gardens. All creatures need water for survival, and the addition of a water feature to any landscape is a sure way to attract birds, butterflies, bullfrogs, and other wildlife to the backyard.

Water features of all kinds—with or without fish, in the house or out in the garden, filled with plants or little more than a basin of still water reflecting the sky—add a soothing element to any setting. The sound of a trickling fountain or cascading waterfall is a compelling element in the landscape—beckoning you to explore and inviting you to relax, if only for a few moments, to forget the day's worries. Gentle gurgles and soft splashes can help mask the sounds of a modern world filled with ringing phones, rumbling traffic, and roaring mowers. If we close our eyes, we just might be transported to a quiet spot beside a mountain stream or to the crystal clear pools beneath a tropical waterfall. A wall spout or tiered fountain can make a courtyard seem 10 degrees cooler on a blistering hot summer day, and a tiny tabletop fountain can bring the atmosphere of the garden indoors.

Although water gardens can take the form of striking architectural waterworks or expansive naturalistic ponds complete with recirculating streams and waterfalls, what I appreciate about water gardens is that anyone can have one, and at little or no expense. It's truly as simple as filling any interesting nonporous container with water and placing it thoughtfully in the landscape where it can reflect the spring flowers, summer skies, and fall foliage. A single floating plant or cut flower can add the perfect finishing touch.

Or a small, inexpensive fountain can be added for the sound of running water. Often, restraint is the key to designing the most attractive water features.

Thanks to advances in technology that have made submersible pumps smaller, more affordable, and easier to operate, many water features now can be assembled in an afternoon or come ready-made from the store shelf—just fill them with water and plug them into a nearby outlet. Preformed and flexible pond liners have, at the same time, simplified the construction and maintenance of garden ponds. Plant breeders have introduced a plethora of garden plants in compact sizes ideally suited to the home water garden. And specialty nurseries and water gardening stores have sprung up throughout the country offering a wide variety of plants, fountains, pumps, and other water gardening supplies.

The goal of this book is to provide inspiration. While there are many how-to books on the market, *Water Garden Idea Book* is about creating a relaxing environment with water features—where to place them in the home and landscape and how to complement them with appropriate plantings. In addition, we have provided a series of drawings that show how basic types of water features are constructed so that you can design plans that suit your style, environment, and budget. Most of all, we hope that the photographs of hundreds of different water features from across the country will spark your imagination. Whether it's a simple water-filled basin, a quiet reflecting pool, a dramatic courtyard cascade, or a fishpond for the grandkids, there's a perfect water feature for every home and garden.

Simple Basins

AH, THE BEAUTY OF SIMPLICITY! All it takes is a modest basin of water to make a big splash in even the smallest of spaces. Water basins are also ideal in larger landscapes, bringing a sense of intimacy to a sunny corner or reflecting a world of passing clouds on a crisp, fall afternoon. With or without plants, a bowl or basin adds an element of intrigue to any garden and will attract wildlife to even the most urban locales.

As long as it holds water, any type of container can work for a water feature—be it a wooden barrel, a dimpled stone, an elegant urn, an old sink, or even a cattle watering trough. Simply select a basin that suits your home's architecture, the surrounding landscape, or your personal style. The real key to designing with basins is making their placement look intentional, not haphazard. Use them as focal points in a garden or to mark transitional areas to gates and paths, or subtly tuck them into a shady border. They are suitable on tabletops, on windowsills, or combined with plant-filled containers on a patio or deck.

◄ A BIRDBATH PLAYS A SUPPORTING ROLE in this garden, attracting wildlife but allowing flowering shrubs and the more prominent gazebo to take center stage. The birdbath's dark color allows it to visually recede and blend into the surroundings.

Bowls and Basins

NO MATTER THE SIZE YOUR GARDEN, there's a place for a bowl, basin, or birdbath. Reflecting the sky above, a basin of still water can make a small garden feel larger. Placed in a border, a brightly colored bowl or water jar can accent plantings. Mounted on a pedestal, a birdbath will attract feathered friends, creating a lovely view that can be enjoyed from indoors as well if placed near a window.

Start by selecting a unique container. If you choose a garden pot, seal the holes with corks and silicone caulk; waterproof boxes and baskets using a flexible pond liner. For the best reflections, choose a container with a dark-colored interior. Then place it in a sunny spot where it will highlight something of interest—perhaps delicate flower blossoms, striking architecture, colorful fall leaves, or the branching pattern of a tree in winter. Small bowls and basins can even be moved around to highlight different features as the seasons change.

▲ FAUX BOULDERS, readily available in many home and garden centers, are an ecological alternative to real stone and much lighter for maneuvering around the landscape. This one marks a transition in the garden where two paths cross.

▼ SKYLIGHT GLIMMERS off this carved granite basin, brightening an otherwise shady corner of the landscape. The tall ornamental grasses that surround the basin not only make for interesting reflections, they provide protective cover for wildlife that is attracted to the basin.

▲ CAREFULLY TUCKED AMONG contrasting foliage, this round basin clearly illustrates the beauty of simplicity and restraint in composition. The simple, worn-looking concrete basin is an important design element, providing a subtle focal point amid the textural ground covers.

▲ POSITIONED AMONG CONTAINERS, this handcrafted, stained-concrete basin and sphere add a sculptural accent to a terrace. Foliage spilling over into the basin provides wispy reflections, and the nasturtium petals float in the water as they drop from the plant.

▲ IN PHOENIX'S DESERT CLIMATE, these rainwater-filled stones serve as a perfect example of naturally occurring water features utilized in a strategic way. The stones edge a gravel driveway, creating a subtle transition between the planted and more utilitarian areas of the landscape.

▶ IN THIS DROUGHT-TOLERANT SANTA FE GARDEN, dimpled stones create ephemeral water features. Due to limited rainfall, rapid evaporation, and tight restrictions on water use, the stones remain dry most of the year. But wet or dry, they add an attractive element to this backyard garden.

◄ FLOATING A SINGLE FLOWER BLOSSOM OR A LARGE LEAF, like this plume poppy leaf, in a basin is a great way to call attention to still water. In even the most imperceptible breeze, the leaf or flower will move about, creating motion in the garden.

◄ JUST ONE WATER LETTUCE PLANT WILL SPREAD to fill this basin with a mass of attractive foliage in a single season. In this Pacific Northwest garden, it is grown safely as an annual, but in several hot-climate states, it has been banned for its invasive tendencies.

WATERPROOF PLANTS

Tropicals

Many favorite water garden plants are tropicals—plants from tropical climates that thrive in the summer heat, but won't survive winter in most North American gardens. They often have spectacular foliage or exotic flowers, so they make great seasonal additions to a water garden. With special care, many can be overwintered in a greenhouse or basement.

Aquatic fern	(*Salvinia* spp.)
Black taro	(*Colocasia esculenta* 'Illustris')
Calla lily	(*Zantedeschia aethiopica*)
Dwarf papyrus	(*Cyperus profiler* 'Nanus')
Green taro	(*Colocasia esculenta* 'Fontanesii')
Mosaic plant	(*Ludwigia sedioides*)
Tropical waterlilies	(*Nymphaea* cvs.)
Water clover	(*Marsilea* spp.)
Water hyssop	(*Bacopa caroliniana*)
Water lettuce	(*Pistia stratiotes*)*
Water poppy	(*Hydrocleys nymphoides*)

* Classified as invasive or potentially invasive in AL, AZ, CA, CT, FL, and SC; never release water garden plants into the wild in any state.

▲ GREEN TARO AND DWARF PAPYRUS fill this lightweight, fiberglass container, which spends the summer on a wooden deck. When cold weather arrives in this New England garden, the water is emptied, the pot is stored in the shed, and the plants are overwintered in the basement.

▲ CARVED STONES OF VARY-ING HEIGHTS are clustered amid a flora-filled front yard to create a one-of-a-kind sculptural element. Two of the three stones are shallow basins that fill with water after a rain. Time-worn river pebbles are exposed as the water level recedes.

Controlling Algae

ALGAE ARE PLANTS THAT DEVELOP naturally in water gardens. Unfortunately, they tend to spread rapidly and can cloud the water, especially when exposed to sunshine and nutrients. Introducing fish, snails, and plants will help keep algae under control. Fish and snails will eat algae, while plants will help keep the water shaded. If adding plants, choose an aquatic growing medium that is low in soluble nutrients. For water features without fish, snails, or plants, adding barley (which comes in bags or small bales) or an organic algaecide can help. If algae gets out of control, it's best to empty and scrub the container (without cleansers), then refill it with fresh water.

◄ ▼ GLIMPSED THROUGH A PARTIALLY OPENED GATE, this small water basin offers an element of intrigue and draws visitors toward the garden beyond. In doing so, it makes this narrow side yard—a neglected space in most landscapes—an inviting destination.

◄ A SIMPLE, WATER-FILLED BASIN placed in open sunshine will reflect the sky and help create a quiet, contemplative mood in any garden. This one is made from hammered copper, which also exhibits exceptional reflective qualities.

Lotuses

The large, fragrant flowers of lotuses are showstoppers. Though these flowers only last a few days, lotuses are equally revered for their parasol-like foliage and dramatic, flat-topped seedpods. They range in height from 2 feet to 8 feet. Although they prefer full sun, lotuses will tolerate some shade in hot climates. Plant them in submerged tubs with only a few inches of water over their growing tips, and feed them with aquatic plant fertilizer tablets. These are a few of the more commonly available lotus varieties:

American lotus	*Nelumbo lutea*
Angel Wings lotus	*Nelumbo* 'Angel Wings'*
Baby Doll lotus	*Nelumbo* 'Baby Doll'*
Charles Thomas lotus	*Nelumbo* 'Charles Thomas'*
Double rose lotus	*Nelumbo* 'Rosea plena'
Empress lotus	*Nelumbo* 'Empress'
Green Maiden lotus	*Nelumbo* 'Green Maiden'
Lavender Lady lotus	*Nelumbo* 'Lavender Lady'
Magnolia lotus	*Nelumbo* 'Alba grandiflora'
Momo Botan lotus	*Nelumbo* 'Momo Botan'*
Mrs. Perry D. Slocum lotus	*Nelumbo* 'Mrs. Perry D. Slocum'
Sacred lotus	*Nelumbo nucifera*
The President lotus	*Nelumbo* 'The President'
Tulip lotus	*Nelumbo* 'Shirokunshi'*

* Small plants especially suited for container water gardens.

▲ PLACED IN A PARTIALLY SHADED BORDER, this large, glossy pot with its umbrella-like lotus leaves held high on stems creates an eye-catching contrast to the surrounding mass of delicate ferns and flowering perennials. The lotus leaves dance about the garden on a breezy day.

◄ THE BASIN ITSELF can be an important design element in a garden, setting the tone or signifying a unique design style. This tall Japanese wash basin, or *chozubachi*, along with the simple lawn chair echo the Asian-style simplicity of the fence and bamboo.

▼ ▶ WHITE AND OTHER LIGHT COLORS easily catch the eye in any landscape. Despite its diminutive size, this light-colored basin stands out against the darker green foliage of azaleas, grasses, and ground covers. Its smooth, flat surface contrasts nicely with its rough sides and the surrounding textured foliage, as does the round cavity against the square base.

BIRDBATHS

▲ SET BACK FROM THE EDGE of a colorful mixed border, this birdbath is safer for birds than if it were placed on a lawn. The surrounding plants act as a deterrent to cats and other predators while rustling foliage alerts birds to approaching company.

◀ WHEN PLACED NEXT TO A WINDOW, a birdbath will provide hours of bird-watching entertainment from indoors. Situating the birdbath inches away from the house and surrounding it with lush greens will make the birds feel right at home while giving you a front row seat.

▲ IF YOU'VE EVER OBSERVED A PET PARAKEET or had cardinals nest in your yard, you know that birds love reflections. Visiting birds will be just as enthralled by their reflections in the mirror placed next to this birdbath as the rusty roadrunner appears to be.

◀ THIS BIRDBATH IS THE CENTERPIECE and focal point of a carefully tended, semiformal garden. Surrounding the birdbath with paving rather than plants calls attention to its shape and integral role in the design of the garden.

◄ STANDING TALL above a mass of pachysandra and against an evergreen backdrop of rhododendron, this concrete birdbath is easily spotted by birds. The dense plantings and raised pedestal create a safe haven for birds to drink and bathe.

► THE DARK INTERIOR OF THIS UN-USUAL, sculptural birdbath brilliantly reflects the dappled light and unforgettable falling blossoms of a golden chain tree (*Laburnum anagyroides*).

Luring Wildlife

Among the joys of water gardening is the wildlife that water attracts. Birds, butterflies, newts, frogs, and turtles are common sights in and around water features. So are dragonflies and damselflies, with their bright bodies and lacy wings. Toads will lay their eggs in the water but spend the rest of their time on dry land. And a water garden (more so ponds than small basins or fountains) may even attract an occasional deer, snake, or raccoon.

Birds, especially, have an affinity for water. They will both drink the water and splash in it to clean their feathers. Provide food and shelter as well, and birds will appear with greater frequency and may make your backyard their home or regular stopping place.

▲ TO ATTRACT DRAGONFLIES (shown here) and damselflies, don't forget to incorporate plants. Roots provide an underwater habitat for nymphs, while foliage offers adults a resting place.

▼ BULLFROGS, WHICH GROW UP TO 6 INCHES LONG, are common throughout much of the country and, along with other frogs and toads, will seek out water features of all kinds.

► BIRDS PREFER A SHALLOW, tapered basin, no more than 3 inches deep in the center, and a rough surface on which they can stand. This tile mosaic birdbath provides the right function and decoration in the landscape.

▼ THE SOUND OF WATER will catch the attention of birds in flight and add serenity to your landscape. Here, a dripper has been attached to the birdbath, dramatically increasing the avian activity in this quaint, front-yard cottage garden.

► THINK OF THE WATER ITSELF AS A DESIGN ELEMENT— providing color, texture, and shape to a garden's composition. This bold, geometric pool of water provides a strong contrasting element in a garden filled with more naturally occurring shapes.

◄ BIRDBATHS STAND OUT VISUALLY when placed against a solid backdrop such as a lawn, fence, or evergreen hedge. Looking from the driveway toward the house, this birdbath is silhouetted against a lighter background, making its form clearly defined.

▼ BIRDBATHS ARE AVAILABLE in a wide range of styles, require very little maintenance, and help create a haven for birds, making them an excellent choice for a first water feature. This one is copper, and adds a subtle touch of elegance to a flourishing garden.

Container Water Gardens

A CONTAINER WATER GARDEN IS NO DIFFERENT from other container plantings except that the plants you choose must thrive in a wet environment. So design a container water garden as you might any other garden container—perhaps with a tall plant in the center, trailing plants overhanging the edges, and midsized filler plants in between.

For a strong vertical accent, add cattails, horsetails, reeds, rushes, or even a lotus. For a softer look, try floating plants such as azola, salvinia, frogbit, and white snowflake. Or keep it simple, with a single, floating plant accenting the container—a dwarf water lily is ideal. Stage plants at different heights based on the depth of the container, the size of the plants, and their individual needs—some like to be waterlogged while others simply prefer damp feet or to float on the water's surface.

▲ EVEN A TINY CAST-IRON TUB or pot can host an attractive water garden. This one is filled with the swordlike foliage of variegated sweet flag (*Acorus calamus* 'Variegatus') and the hooded leaves of yellow pitcher plant (*Sarracenia flava*).

◄ ATTICS, ANTIQUE STORES, AND FLEA MARKETS are excellent places to find unusual basins. The marble basin mounted on this Rhode Island barn is filled with a pot of variegated sweet flag. The yellow in its leaves echoes the spots on the encroaching leopard plant.

20

▲ CONTRAST LEAF AND FLOWER SHAPES for a striking planting. Here, tall, narrow cattails (*Typha laxmannii*) and variegated spider lily (*Hymenocallis caribaea* 'Variegata') contrast with broad-leaved water lettuce (*Pistia stratiotes*), cranberry taro (*Colocasia rubra*), and water lilies (*Nymphaea* spp.).

◄ THIS BROAD, HEAVY CONTAINER is next to impossible to tip over, especially once filled with water, making it an ideal choice for a high-traffic area. It can also hold many more plants than an upright container of equal volume.

► PLANT BREEDERS HAVE INTRODUCED compact varieties of plants that are suitable for container water gardens. The dwarf lotus (*Nelumbo* spp.), whose broad leaves extend high on stems, is a good example. Here it is paired with the grasslike shoots and white flowers of star sedge (*Rhynchospora colorata*).

Staging Plants

The planting depths of water garden plants vary by type. Only the roots of marginal plants can tolerate moisture, while submerged plants must remain completely covered by water. Many floating plants aren't planted at all; they simply float freely on the water's surface. For this reason, water garden plants must be staged at different depths, whether in a container or pond. Depending on the pot size and shape and the depth of the water, plants may be placed either on the floor or raised on supports such as bricks, concrete blocks, or overturned terra-cotta pots. In many cases, shelves can be built into the walls of a water feature or straddled across supports to hold more plants.

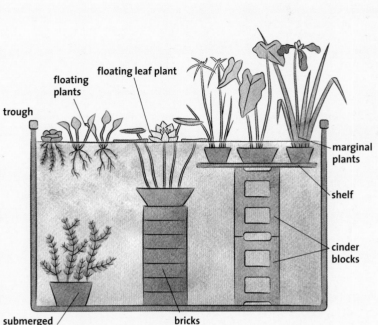

► CONTAINER WATER GARDENS are ideal for decks where they can be easily viewed from indoors or will accent an outdoor seating area. This one is made from a cattle trough—which costs considerably less than a ceramic or terra-cotta pot half its size.

◄ RECYCLED OBJECTS FROM AROUND THE HOUSE can turn a container water garden into a favorite conversation piece. This old claw-foot tub finds renewed life as a home for water-loving rushes, sedges, and irises. The unique dragonfly sculpture adds to the distinctive charm.

▲ THIS LARGE CAULDRON ANCHORS a flagstone patio that extends out into the sun-drenched lawn—a location much appreciated by the majority of water garden plants, which need at least five to six hours of sun a day to thrive.

Mosquito Control

MOSQUITOES CAN PUT A DAMPER on any garden party. Fortunately, they can also be controlled. Replacing the water in a shallow basin twice a week will help, as mosquito larvae hatch in a week. Nontoxic mosquito-control dunks (which look like small donuts) can be added to the water. Goldfish or mosquito fish will eat the mosquito larvae while adding interest to a water garden. Installing a small fountain to keep the water moving is also a good option, as mosquitoes only lay their eggs in still water. Even a small dripper can be attached to birdbaths; it will deter mosquitoes while attracting feathered friends.

▲ THIS IRIS-FILLED CERAMIC POT can remain outdoors year-round in its moderate California climate. In places where temperatures drop below freezing, such pots should be emptied for the winter to prevent cracking, but the iris may remain outdoors.

▲ MIX-AND-MATCH WATER FEATURES. This compact garden has four: a unique blue basin with a dwarf water lily, a bubbling urn, a naturalistic pond, and a trickling fountain along the pond's edge. Combined, the variety of features draws you deep into the garden.

Soothing Fountains

T HE VERY SOUNDS OF WATER—trickling, gurgling, splashing, dripping, lapping, bubbling—can help calm jangled nerves, set the mood for a romantic al fresco dinner, or lull you into gentle sleep. Indoors and out, the sound of water can transform a home into a peaceful haven, but when used outdoors, it also helps to mask neighborhood noises—passing traffic, mowers and blowers, ringing phones, and barking dogs.

The quickest and easiest way to introduce the sound of water into the landscape is by installing a fountain. Fountains may be formal structures that relate to architectural elements of the home, or they may settle more naturally into their surroundings, carefully tucked among plantings. In their simplest form, fountains are little more than recirculating water forced through a tube, pipe, or nozzle. Yet they can spurt, spout, cascade, fall, or bubble for infinite variety. The water in fountains will sparkle in sunlight, dance in the wind, and shimmer after dark beneath outdoor lighting.

◄ BUBBLING URNS AND FOUNTAINS are a good choice for small water gardens, as they create just enough water movement to aerate the water and deter mosquitoes without disturbing the plants. This helps maintain a healthy, balanced environment in the pond.

Spouting Fountains

WHETHER PULSATING PLUMES OF WATER dancing high above a reflecting pool or a spurting statuary frog perched on the edge of a pond, spouting fountains put on a show for all to see and hear. Most can be easily added to existing water features and can be as simple as a submersible pump and pipe through which water is forced for a natural, geyser effect; others may have a nozzle at the end of the pipe that sprays the water out in a pattern. Flow-control valves on pumps can be adjusted to alter the spray's height or spread. Statuary fountains, which come in styles to suit any garden, are generally placed at the water's edge or on a pedestal above the water. Some spouting fountains are even available as self-contained units that are filled with water and plugged into a nearby outlet.

▲ SPOUTING STATUARY fountains come in all shapes and sizes, and can accompany any basin or body of water. This verdigris frog sits aside a raised pool and creates an eye-catching display as it splashes against these colorful spheres and into the water.

◄ THE HIGHER THE WATER PRESSURE, the faster this double-headed sprinkler spins, making fanciful water patterns in the air. It is best suited for watering lawns but also offers kids (of all ages) a fun way to cool off on a hot summer day.

▲ WHAT LOOKS LIKE AN ANTIQUE KETTLE used for boiling sugar cane is actually an inexpensive steel bowl raised above the water level on a steel grid. It was powder coated (a dry-paint application that is more durable than wet paint) a dark color for an aged appearance.

▲ **ALTHOUGH THIS WATER FEATURE** runs only when the garden is thirsty, there's no reason why you can't transform a sprinkler into an entertaining water feature that runs continuously in a pond. Look for one of a variety of new sprinklers with unique heads and spray patterns.

Statuary Fountain in a Trough

Small statuary-style fountains that are placed in basins or ponds are among the easiest to install. Often, they are sold as kits, with pumps and fittings included. If not, the pump, connecting tube, and fittings can be purchased separately and assembled. Choose a pump with an electrical cord long enough to reach the nearest GFCI outlet, or plan to install an outlet near the pump. Place the pump in the deepest part of the basin, and be sure the water level doesn't drop below the pump intake valve, which would cause the motor to burn out.

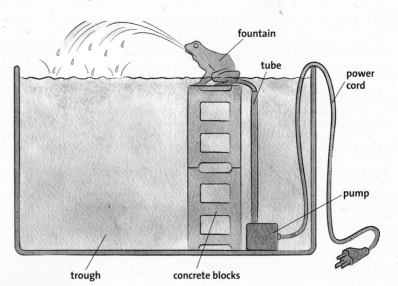

fountain

tube

power cord

pump

trough

concrete blocks

◀ SMALL, INEXPENSIVE FOUNTAINS can be tucked in among plants inside container water gardens or ponds. This one sits atop a couple of concrete blocks for support and is attached to a small pump by tubing. The pump plugs into a nearby outlet for power.

◀ THIS SWAN FOUNTAIN is located in a raised bed just a few feet from the front door. Although it is close enough to plug into a wall outlet, it was wired by an electrician so the pump could be switched on and off from indoors.

Creating a Garden Room

To CREATE A GARDEN ROOM, think in terms of walls, floors, ceilings, and passageways—just like a room in a house. Walls can be created with traditional materials as well as fences, lattice, hedges, or mixed planting beds. They may be 6 feet tall or more for privacy, or little more than a foot high to create a sense of enclosure while allowing views in and out of the garden room. In many cases, mixing two or more wall heights provides privacy without isolation.

Floors can be made from a range of materials as well—stone, brick, gravel, and concrete pavers are all excellent low-maintenance choices. Grass is also an option, though in a garden room with furniture, it may be difficult to mow. For the ceiling, an open sky may be just the ticket. For shade, consider the canopy of a tree, a vine-covered arbor, or even sailcloth panels strung overhead. Passageways may simply be narrow openings in the garden wall, or they may be marked by gates, arbors, posts, pots, or changes in grade.

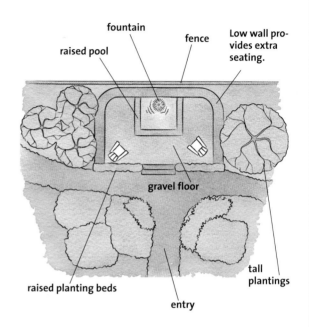

fountain

fence

Low wall provides extra seating.

raised pool

gravel floor

raised planting beds

entry

tall plantings

▲ SET AGAINST A BACKYARD FENCE, this fountain presented the perfect opportunity to create a small garden room. Just large enough for a couple of chairs, it provides a cozy retreat on a nearly 1-acre lot. The raised pool edge offers additional seating.

▲ DOLPHIN FOUNTAINS, symbolizing the dolphin fish (mahi-mahi) rather than the porpoise, date back to Roman times. This one leaps from the water, drawing attention to the round, raised fishpond that was built into a gently curving stone retaining wall.

◄ THIS WATER FEATURE is located midway along a watercourse in a steep side-yard garden. Because the water ultimately flows downhill, the force of gravity, rather than a pump, moves the water through the whimsical fountain.

◄ ▼ THE SOUND OF SPLASHING WATER sends a compelling invitation that cannot be denied. Guests never visit this garden without being tempted beyond the courtyard doors. There, they are treated to a long, axial view of the garden and this enchanting pool, which features a traditional statuary fountain and is embraced by a circular boxwood hedge.

Floating Plants

Floating plants play a key role in water garden ecology. They lower water temperature by covering the water surface, creating a less hospitable environment for algae. Some simply float on the surface; others have roots anchored in submerged pots. The biggest challenge is controlling the spread of many floating plants. For a healthy ecosystem, don't allow them to cover more than 70 percent of the water's surface. Here are some of the most popular floating plants for water gardens:

Common duckweed	(*Lemna minor*)
Floating heart	(*Nymphoides* spp.)
Fairy moss	(*Azolla caroliniana*)
Frogbit	(*Hydrocharis morsus-ranae*)
Pond lily	(*Nuphar* spp.)
Water hawthorn	(*Aponogeton distachyus*)
Water hyacinth	(*Eichhornia crassipes*)*
Water lily	(*Nymphaea* spp.)

* Due to its invasive tendencies, this plant should not be grown in AL, AZ, CA, CT, FL, SC, or TX, and should never be released into the wild in any state.

▲ BAMBOO FOUNTAINS typically spill into wash basins, but this one flows into a container water garden featuring a floating, textured mass of fairy moss (*Azolla filiculoides*) amid stands of yellow flag iris (*Iris pseudacorus*) and papyrus (*Cyperus papyrus*).

◀ THIS WHIMSICAL SPRINKLER HEAD puts on a spectacular show in a pond while serving a very practical role of aerating the water. It is mounted atop a sturdy copper tube that is attached to a recirculating, underwater pump.

A Simple Spray Fountain

Spray fountains, which consist of a pump and outlet pipe, can be installed in containers, larger basins, pools, and ponds. A natural-looking geyser is created when the pipe is cut off near the water level, but the pipe can also be fitted with various nozzles to create spray patterns.

The height of the water shooting into the air is determined by several factors: the size of the pump, the diameter of the pipe, the flow of the water (which can be controlled by a valve on the pump or pipe), and the nozzle selected.

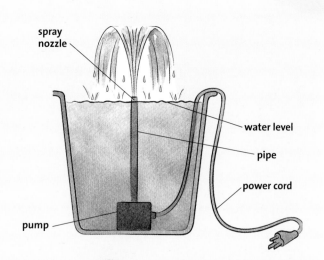

spray nozzle

water level

pipe

power cord

pump

bell

bubble

tiered

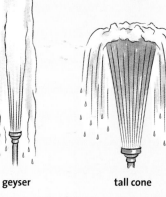

geyser

tall cone

short cone

ring

▶ THIS SPINNING SPRINKLER shoots water nearly 10 feet in the air and makes a soft spattering sound on the water. Though small in size, the sprinkler creates a broad water pattern (roughly 6 feet across) that is best suited to midsize and large garden ponds.

◀ SIMPLY DESIGNED AND CAREFULLY CRAFTED, this hammered copper fountain complements the craftsman-style architecture of the house and adjacent studio. It was added during a renovation project that included the creation of this small courtyard that marks the transition between the front entry, studio, and backyard.

▶ A TINY BOWL, A TINY FOUNTAIN, and a tiny pump—that's all it takes to create a refreshingly simple water feature that is small enough to fit into any garden. Even this Buddha seems soothed by the sound.

Cascading Fountains

ASCADING FOUNTAINS ARE SIMILAR TO SPOUTING fountains but instead of forcing the water upward or outward through the air, they pump the water up through a pipe and allow the force of gravity to carry it back into the reservoir. Cascading fountains such as tiered fountains and many hanging wall fountains may be self-contained with the fountain, basin, pump, and plumbing in a single fixture. More often, they are created by combining elements—perhaps a series of stacked tubs or urns, or a decorative wall spout with a separate basin below.

Wall fountains are ideal positioned against a courtyard wall but can look at home against any wall, outdoors or indoors. Traditional tiered fountains lend themselves to a more formal landscape, while statuary fountains come in a range of styles and materials that are suited to a variety of environments from classic to contemporary.

▶ THIS ELOQUENT STATUARY pairs with the sound of water and the sweet fragrance of roses to create a classic garden scene. Sweet-smelling flowers are a nice accent near fountains, since they encourage passersby to stop and enjoy the sights, sounds, and fragrance.

◀ DENSE PLANTINGS partially screen this cast-concrete fountain, which is tucked into a side border along a curving garden path. Like a raven, it is heard long before it is seen, drawing visitors through the garden. The water trickles through bricks into a small underground basin.

▲ THIS CONCRETE COLUMN WAS PLACED to the west of the patio so that the setting sun would shine through the falling water each evening. For those who enjoy their morning coffee outdoors, positioning a water feature to the east would produce similar results.

◄ A FLOWER SERVED as the inspiration for this fountain. The six triangular pieces of cut bluestone were carefully assembled to represent six flower petals, and the water spout symbolizes the flower's pistil. Water drains between the petals into a concrete basin.

▼ THIS ORGANIC-LOOKING FOUNTAIN blends right in with the surrounding plants. With the pump set on low flow, water spills over a stained-concrete form that was cast from a real (and very large) gunnera leaf, then trickles slowly into the pond.

Altering the Sound of Water

THE TONE AND INTENSITY of falling water is easily altered. There are no magic formulas, but altering the volume of water, the height from which it falls, the surface over which it falls, and amount of water in the basin all affect the sound quality. The key is scaling the sound to the space and mood. High, spouting fountains make a loud splash, while bubbling stones produce a gentle gurgle. Water spilling directly into a pool makes more noise than water falling onto a mossy stone. Keep in mind that what might suit a broad, open space could easily overwhelm a small courtyard. Likewise, the trickle of a tabletop fountain might be lost outdoors.

▼ SOMETIMES A LITTLE INGENUITY IS REQUIRED to achieve just the right effect. A piece of tin was snipped, bent, and set in this urn to facilitate a smoother flow of water over its edge. From viewing distance in the garden, the tin is not visible.

▲ TERRACING AND A CASCADING WATER FEATURE transformed this steep San Francisco backyard from an impossible-to-mow lawn into a garden that appeals to the senses of sight and sound. The flowing water also does a great job drowning out city noises.

Winterizing a Fountain

IN MILD CLIMATES, fountains can continue running all winter with only routine maintenance to clean the filter and to add water as needed. Where occasional, short freezes are common, it's possible to keep a fountain running as long as basins are deep and water can be added frequently. Stone fountains hold up much better than ceramic fountains under these conditions. Where temperatures frequently dip into the teens or remain below freezing for more than a few days at a time, it's best to drain a fountain and remove the pump for the winter. Water freezes quickly under these conditions, draining a shallow basin rapidly, which could damage the pump. Don't just unplug the pump since any remaining, nonmoving water in the fountain will also begin freeze.

▲ FACETED EDGES, like those cut into this stone, catch light and create shadows. They also vary the flow of water over the edge of the bubbling birdbath. The sound of water falling into the pond is an irregular splash rather than a smooth, steady stream.

▼ THE STONEWORK IN THIS LANDSCAPE gives it character, from the custom birdbath to the unique pool edge and stone bench in the background. The subdued foliage complements the design elements, letting the stone pieces take center stage.

◀ FLANKED BY A WALL of Boston ivy, this small cherub fountain has an old-world feel to it. The scene is equally compelling in fall and winter as the ivy leaves turn to brilliant red, and then drop to expose the intricate weaving of the vine.

▼ THIS CHARMING STATUARY FOUNTAIN is built into the birdbath, so it is completely self-contained and does not require a separate basin. The pump resides in the pedestal.

▲ THIS UNIQUE WATERFALL was carved from a single granite boulder. Water bubbles out the top, ripples over the washboardlike surface, and vanishes into the ground. The hidden reservoir is 4 feet square, 18 inches deep, and sealed with a rubber pond liner.

◄ MOVING PARTS—not just moving water—make this metal water sculpture a showstopper. Each of the three paddles moves at a different speed, creating a variety of sounds as the water hits the metal and splashes into the pool below.

Running Water Spigot

Friends seeing this water feature for the first time will be tempted to turn off the spigot, but the water runs continuously. Relatively simple and inexpensive to construct, it can be built in an afternoon with a hollow post, half barrel, faucet, pump, and a few pieces of plumbing.

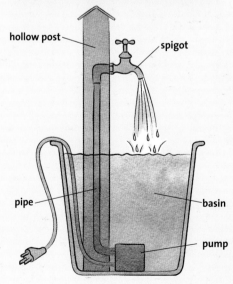

hollow post

spigot

pipe

basin

pump

TIERED FOUNTAINS

► FOUNTAINS MAKE EXCEL-
LENT FOCAL POINTS in any
landscape. This one is visually
framed by an artfully crafted,
rusted-metal arch. A narrow,
mulched path winds past the
fountain and through the
woodland garden, ending at
a small flagstone patio with
seating that overlooks the
water feature.

▲ COPPER BOWLS, with their slightly
metallic ring, make wonderful catch
basins for a tiered fountain. These are
stacked on individual stone pedestals
against a stucco courtyard wall and set
at angles so the water spills out only
on one side.

◄ THE CENTERPIECE OF AN ENTRY
COURTYARD, this two-tiered fountain
is enjoyed by neighbors out for an evening walk. Although the upper basin
bubbles, the water does not spill over
the edge. Instead, it flows through a
series of spouts in the side of the basin.

▲ A FORMAL-STYLE FOUNTAIN takes on a more casual and unique tone when it's created with natural materials. The column of this tiered fountain was made from round soapstone cobbles found on the property. The basins were carved from thick slabs of bluestone.

▶ IN A TRADITIONAL TIERED FOUNTAIN, the pump is placed inside the pedestal at the base of the lowest basin. In this case, the basin is actually a small, round pool. What makes this fountain unique is the addition of floating plants at each level.

◄ IN A VARIATION ON A THEME, the top tier of this fountain is a bubbling sphere rather than a basin. The fountain is placed at the end of a long garden path to draw the eye down the length of the garden.

▲ THIS FOUNTAIN FEATURES seven water elements—a raised pool, birdbath, spurting upright fountain, and four side-mounted spouting fountains. A single pump forces water from the pool up through the fountain and out through the five spouts.

◄ ALL KINDS OF CONTAINERS can be transformed into tiered fountains. Here, water is pumped up through the center urn, which overflows into three urns, which, in turn, continue to spill over because they are already full of water. The overflow splashes to the pool below.

WALL FOUNTAINS

▼ ALTHOUGH IT IS NOT BUILT INTO THE WALL, this freestanding fountain and basin (purchased as a single, self-contained unit) is positioned as a wall fountain would be. The arched trellis helps complete the look of a traditional wall fountain.

NUTS AND BOLTS

Hanging a Wall Fountain

The first rule of thumb in hanging a wall fountain is to select a solid wall. Wood and masonry walls are good choices, and drywall and plaster walls will work as long as the fountain can be hung from studs that will support the weight. Matters are simplified if a power outlet exists or can be installed directly behind the fountain. If this is not possible, plants or trellising may be used to conceal the cord as it runs down the wall and to the nearest outlet. Wiring can also be run through the wall to a nearby switch.

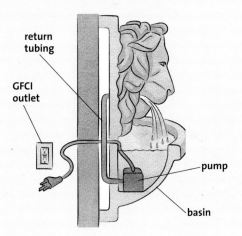

◄ AT FIRST GLANCE, this is a simple bird-bath on a pedestal. More careful inspection reveals a spouting wall fountain in the form of the mysterious "green man" who is often found in gardens. Dense evergreen ivy conceals the return pipes and electrical wires.

▼ THIS WALL FOUNTAIN is actually a freestanding unit placed against a wall. The homeowner installed Mexican tile against the house wall to provide a colorful backdrop for the cascading fountain and basin and to give the appearance of a custom-designed water feature.

▲ THIS WALL FOUNTAIN ADDS AN INTERESTING design element to a simple courtyard wall. The stone façade was built around the fountain for support and to camouflage the plumbing. Water spills into an antique copper basin, which produces a higher pitch than a masonry pool would.

▶ MOUNTED AGAINST A HOUSE WALL near the driveway, this two-piece fountain greets the homeowners with soothing sounds each time they return home. Over time, the copper will take on a green patina.

Spot-Lighting a Fountain

WHEN COMBINED, WATER AND LIGHTS create a magical atmosphere. Lights generate reflections and shadows on still water, while causing moving water to shimmer and sparkle.

If the fountain has a textured surface—perhaps a millstone or chiseled bluestone—strong, narrow beams of cross-lighting from spotlights will accentuate that texture. Spotlights can also be used to create dramatic shadows—such as those falling from a three-dimensional wall fountain. Place one spotlight to the side to highlight texture or to create a single, directional shadow, or use two spotlights (one on either side) to cast shadows in both directions. For cascades, consider placing a low-voltage, waterproof spotlight in or near the basin to shine up into the falling water.

Remember, it's the water feature and not the light itself that should be seen, so conceal any bulbs from view. In addition to encasing bulbs in a fixture to cut down glare, the fixtures can be set between rocks, behind shrubs, or recessed into the ground. All lights should be positioned between the viewing area and water feature, and angled away from any seating or gathering areas. And since water and electricity don't mix, be sure all lighting fixtures and installations meet safety guidelines.

▲ A PAIR OF SMALL UP-LIGHTS hidden amid the ground covers and perennials cast light on this stacked-block fountain. In addition to calling attention to the fountain, the lights emphasize the rough surface texture of the blocks and cast interesting shadows of one block against another.

◄ SPOTLIGHTS PLACED ON EITHER SIDE of this dolphin wall fountain create dramatic shadows against a courtyard wall. When using spotlights, experiment with their position and the length and angle of shadows they create before their final installation.

The Symbolism of Japanese Fountains

WATER IS SYMBOLIC in almost every culture. In Japan, it represents purification. Prior to the tea ceremony, which is more about taking a break to meditate on the important things in life than it is about drinking tea, it is customary to wash the hands and mouth in a small basin outside the tea hut as an act of purifying the mind and body. Short *tsukubai* and taller *chozubachi* basins are made from stone and feature a bamboo spout, or *kakei*. Traditionally, these basins were fed with fresh water. In Western gardens, they may feature recirculating water and be more symbolic than functional. Still, they call us to pause and reflect.

▲ THE FOUNTAIN AND TRAILING COBBLES bring to mind a spring and stream. In reality, the water from this Japanese wash basin flows into a hidden reservoir beneath the cobbles, where it is then pumped back up through the bamboo post and out the spout.

▶ THE *TSUKUBAI*, or crouching water basin, was traditionally used to wash the hands and mouth prior to the tea ceremony as an act of mind and body purification. Here it is paired with a *kakei*, a traditional bamboo fountain, and a bamboo ladle.

▲ ALTHOUGH STONE BASINS WITH BAMBOO FOUNTAINS are more commonly set over a hidden basin of water, it is not unusual to find them surrounded by a symbolic sea of water, especially when their purpose, like this one, is primarily aesthetic.

▲ IN A VERY MODERN TWIST on a very traditional design concept, this one-of-a-kind water feature is notable for its clean lines and distinctive materials. The tall water basin is reminiscent of Japanese *chozubachi*, and the copper pipe is similar in form to a bamboo spout.

◄ THE SMALL SQUARE POND on this patio is accented by a simple bamboo fountain that is in keeping with the Japanese-style tea house and wooden arbor in the rear garden. It helps mark the transition from the house to the garden and sets the stage for a serene atmosphere.

Japanese Deer Scarer

A variation on the popular bamboo fountain is the Japanese deer scarer, or *shishi-odoshi*. The bamboo fountain spout fills a bamboo rocker with water until it tips over, making a hollow knocking sound as it hits the stone basin. It was originally developed by Japanese farmers as a way to scare deer away from their fields.

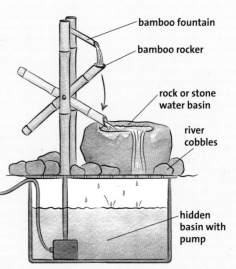

bamboo fountain
bamboo rocker
rock or stone water basin
river cobbles
hidden basin with pump

▲ JAPANESE BASINS vary in materials and height, and can be placed along the edge of a symbolic "sea" or at its center. This low basin surrounded by dry river cobbles occupies a low position in the landscape, much as a natural body of water would.

Bubbling Fountains

BUBBLING WATER FEATURES PROVIDE THE MOST SOOTHING OF SOUNDS. As such, they are ideally suited to small courtyards where sounds tend to bounce off the walls. Because they bubble, rather than splash, they are also appropriate for patios, decks, terraces, and indoor spaces, where surrounding areas must be kept dry.

Bubbling stones are reminiscent of natural springs, and for this reason are often placed in the landscape among plants. Very little water is exposed at any one time, so they make good choices for hot, windy landscapes where water is scarce and local restrictions may apply. They can be made from natural boulders or carved stone, with a hole drilled through the center for water recirculation. Old millstones work well, too, and favorite pots or urns can easily be adapted to create a bubbling water feature. Most often, water basins are hidden below ground, but attractive above-ground basins are also suitable.

▲ THIS TALL, BUBBLING POT adds an upright accent next to the horizontal plane of a swimming pool in a small Florida backyard. The trickling sound of the fountain makes the temperature in this semitropical climate seem just a little bit cooler.

◄ BOXWOODS AND AXIAL VIEWS may give this garden a sense of order, but the round cattle trough basin and iris-filled bubbling urn give it personality. The stepping-stones—large metal tubs filled with concrete—blend right in, echoing the shapes and materials of the fountain.

▲ POSITIONED JUST INSIDE AN ENTRY COURTYARD, this fountain makes a memorable first and last impression by creating a relaxed, welcoming environment for guests who are waiting to be greeted at the front door or lingering over goodbyes on their way home.

▲ EVEN IN EARLY SPRING, before the perennials have filled the garden with color, this courtyard is eye-catching. The bubbling granite sphere anchors an octagonal tile patio, while black cobbles camouflage an underground reservoir. Rusted bird sculptures add a whimsical note to the courtyard.

◄ SPHERES AND OTHER ROUND OBJECTS add formality to any landscape because they contrast with the natural forms around them. The earthy tones in this large bubbling sphere are echoed in the local red soil and nearby silver-foliaged plants.

▶ THERE'S NO HOLE TO DIG with an above-ground reservoir. This basin is smaller than most, but the reduced water flow in a bubbling water feature means there is little splash to contain. The basin is just large enough to house a small pump.

▼ UPRIGHT FOUNTAINS AND BUBBLING STONES, like this one carved from granite, look best when set against a simple, solid backdrop like fences and evergreen plantings. That way, they stand out rather than compete with their surroundings.

Fountain Maintenance

ALTHOUGH MOST FOUNTAINS are fairly easy to maintain, they are not carefree because it is difficult to maintain a balanced environment in any small water feature. Algae growth must be kept in check, and if necessary, a nontoxic algaecide can be used to help control algae growth. Leaves that fall into a fountain should be removed, and pumps should be cleaned at least annually with a hard spray of water to knock away any accumulated muck and debris. In areas with hard water, a water softener designed for fountains will help keep the pump humming along.

◄ THIS BUBBLING BALL BIRDBATH was inspired by a solid sphere already in the garden when one of the home-owners thought aloud, "Wouldn't it be nice if that sphere did something?" The new, bubbling sphere is perched on a terrace wall, attracting birds to the garden.

▲ THIS SCULPTURAL WATER FEATURE serves as a focal point at the end of a path, drawing visitors toward an informal courtyard at the home's entry. Here, it not only sets a relaxed tone for visitors, but can be enjoyed from in-doors when the windows are open.

► THIS EARTH-COLORED BUBBLING URN is the sole man-made focal point along a mulched garden path in a shaded front-yard garden. The simplicity of the naturalistic landscaping and water feature, along with the trickling sound, creates a peaceful setting in this neighborhood.

◄ SMALL BUBBLING STONES with hidden reservoirs are a practical choice for dry climates such as the Southwest, where tight water restrictions exist. Water loss to wind or evaporation is greatly reduced by minimal surface water exposure and little or no splash.

▼ THE CLEAN, SIMPLE LANDSCAPE DESIGN and small bubbling stone help create a serene setting in this Santa Fe courtyard. A similar environment could be created in any small space, perhaps using fences or hedges for the walls.

◄ BOULDERS SHOULD COME FROM SITES destined for development rather than from rivers or other undisturbed natural areas. The contractor who moved this boulder was careful to study its natural placement before it was moved so that it could be similarly repositioned once transformed into a fountain.

▼ OLD MILLSTONES ARE HARD TO FIND, but new ones are available from a variety of sources. This one, hand-carved from granite, is darker in color than most and features a smooth finish. It anchors a colorful fall border in the Southwest.

Bubbling River Stones

Underground basins can be made from any number of materials, but the easiest and least expensive to work with may be a large rubber tub. Dig a hole for the tub so that it can be placed with the rim flush with ground level. Place a small, submersible pump in the bottom, running the power cord out along one side and the return tube straight up, an inch or two above ground level.

Cover the tub with a metal grid that is strong enough to support the stones and that has crossbars spaced close enough to keep stones from falling through. (As an alternative, a layer of mesh can be placed atop the crossbars. Fountain kits with a pre-assembled basin and grid are also available.) If possible, fabricate a "trap door" in one corner so that the pump filter can be cleaned periodically without having to lift the entire grid. Run the fountain pipe up through the grid and conceal both the grid and pipe with river cobbles. Fill the basin approximately two-thirds full with water, making sure to cover the pump by at least several inches. Finally, plug in the pump and check the water level weekly.

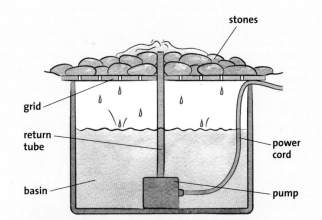

◀ ▲ THESE BUBBLING STONES create a sense of mystery in the garden, bringing to mind a spring or geyser. That atmosphere is enhanced by the feature's low-profile placement at the back of a densely planted, in-town garden where one must seek it out.

◄ THE RESERVOIR FOR THIS FOUNTAIN was built on the ground, and a low deck was built around it to create a cozy outdoor room along the side of the house. The fountain was carved from local stone, so it suits this southwestern landscape well.

▼ THE DEEPLY CUT TEXTURE of this Etruscan urn fountain is accentuated in early morning and late afternoon, when light from the low sun angles across its surface. Dappled light created by nearby trees also helps to create an appealing effect.

▲ THIS FOUNTAIN WAS CUT from Colorado granite and placed in a shady corner beneath a house window. The ferns and sweet flag were allowed to grow all the way up to the edge of the stone and basin to soften its hard surfaces.

▲ BOTH SCULPTURE AND WATER FEATURE, this bubbling stone is given a prominent position in the landscape by placing it amid the lawn with a light-colored courtyard wall as the backdrop. This ensures that it can be easily viewed from the house and patio.

▶ MIX AND MATCH to create a fountain. This sphere and container were sold as a kit, but they could have been created from separate elements. Though this fountain overflows into an underground basin, the container itself could serve as a basin for the bubbling sphere.

Wiring Basics

ALL RECIRCULATING WATER FEATURES require a pump, and all pumps require power. That's not a problem if your water feature is just a few feet from a GFCI outlet. Sometimes, you can buy a pump with extra length of cord. However, because water and electricity don't mix, extension cords aren't a safe option for extended outdoor use. Hire an electrician to install a small GFCI outlet with a switch just a few feet from your water feature, and then camouflage it with shrubbery. Better yet, have your electrician install a switch in the house so you can control your water feature from indoors. Another option for small fountains is to use a low-voltage pump that can be run from a transformer through buried lines that you can install yourself.

▲ THIS NARROW BACKYARD on a corner lot is only about 10 feet deep, but that's plenty of room for a small outdoor dining patio with a table for two. The bubbling stone provides soft background music.

◄ PLACED IN THE MIDDLE OF A BROAD PATH that leads to the front door, this gently bubbling urn offers a welcoming sight and sound to arriving guests. Nearby benches provide a place to linger.

◄ ▲ MILLSTONES ARE EASILY CONVERTED to bubbling fountains because water can be pumped up through their center cog. The water then runs out along the grooves in the millstone's surface. This millstone fountain was carefully tucked among hostas, a Japanese maple, and other plants that partially screen it from view to create an element of intrigue in this small courtyard. It's located just outside the back door, within easy ear-shot of the patio.

▲ THE MUTED COLORS AND CRACKED SURFACE of this urn, along with the moss-covered bricks and dense, rambling plantings, give this bubbling fountain a well-established look. Moss can be encouraged by rubbing a bit of buttermilk over the surface of new bricks.

◄ CERAMIC POTS MAKE EXCELLENT WATER FEATURES. Many already have drainage holes, which make installing a fountain pipe easy. If not, drill a hole with a masonry bit. The real trick is making sure the pot rim is level so water flows evenly over the edge.

▶ IN THIS CLASSIC URN, water is forced up through a pipe that protrudes just barely above water level, calling attention to the water rather than the pipe. The pressure has been adjusted to create a noticeable spout without losing significant water to spray or splashing.

▼ A BUBBLER WITH A TWIST, this helix fountain has deeply carved segments that alter the flow of water over its surface. Heavy fountains, such as this granite column, should be set on a concrete pedestal (inside the basin) for support.

▲ DEEP-SEA-BLUE POTS with a wavy surface are a befitting choice for a water feature. This one is enhanced by using two pots instead of one. Each operates as a separate fountain, but they share a single large basin.

INDOOR FOUNTAINS

▶ NOT ALL INDOOR WATER FEATURES are tabletop models. Some hang on walls and others, like
this stone sphere and chiseled stone basin, are set
atop pedestals. Like most indoor fountains, the
unit is self-contained.

▼ THE SAME ELEMENTS used for outdoor bubbling
features can be adapted indoors, though usually on
a much smaller scale. This bubbling copper sphere
is small enough to sit on a tabletop, and the aging
verdigris adds a colorful note not generally found
in stone.

◄ WATER FEATURES TEND TO BE THE CENTER of attention outdoors, while fireplaces are the strongest draw indoors. Here, the role is reversed. Instead of a fireplace, this house wall features a sleek bubbling fountain. A shallow water basin was built into the home's slab flooring.

▼ TABLETOP FOUNTAINS CAN BE COMBINED with other elements, such as the raku pottery pots atop this chest, to create an interesting ornamental accent in a room. Here, the sound adds a calming note to a dining area.

◄ WATER FEATURES CAN BE SCULPTURAL or even architectural elements in the home and are appropriate for any room. Water lightly tumbles down the side of this pyramid through a small slot and into a hidden basin.

Naturalistic Ponds and Streams

IMITATING NATURE BY BUILDING PONDS, STREAMS, AND WATERFALLS in the landscape is an effective way to bring beauty and serenity to any backyard. The most natural-looking water features are irregularly shaped and use natural materials in subtle rather than contrived ways. But don't be fooled. Naturalistic ponds and streams don't just happen. It can actually be challenging to create a scheme as if Mother Nature had her hand in its design. Boulders, for instance, are best randomly clustered and partially buried rather than stacked uniformly. Sand, pebbles, or decomposing leaves that fill gaps between the boulders, and plants that are allowed to grow all the way into the water rather than stopping at the water's edge contribute to the naturalistic feel. And streams meandering along a curving route rather than flowing in a straight line, with the originating point of water carefully concealed by boulders and plants, might even fool Mother Nature herself.

Large ponds are easier to maintain than small ones, but without fresh water flowing into them continuously, no pond can establish a healthy, balanced ecosystem on its own. Fortunately, plants and fish can help, but pumps, fountains, filters, and water additives will also be needed to maintain a level of water quality that is appealing to both wildlife and garden visitors.

◄ THESE IRREGULARLY SIZED AND PLACED BOULDERS are both more natural looking and more interesting than similarly sized rocks placed uniformly around a pond. By leaving gaps along the edges, marginal plants are allowed to grow all the way down to and into the water.

Garden Ponds

SELECTING THE RIGHT LOCATION is an important first step in pond design. In nature, ponds form naturally at low points in the landscape where water accumulates. In the designed landscape, however, there should always be a lower point where rainwater runoff and pond overflow can go to help keep fertilizers, herbicides, and other debris from flowing into the pond.

Most flowering water plants prefer six to eight hours of sun a day while fish prefer some shade. So rather than worry about sun or shade, place a pond where it can be seen and enjoyed. If the spot is shady, many foliage plants will still thrive in the pond. If it's sunny, simply cover much of the water's surface with plants or rock ledges to create shade for fish. An added benefit to this approach: algae growth will be minimized.

▲ PERFECTLY POSITIONED, this small pond is neither the high point nor low point in a gently sloping backyard. The dense plantings and carefully shaped terrain around the pond direct runoff to other locations in the landscape, which help maintain a healthy water environment for goldfish.

▲ TUCKED BETWEEN A CAMELIA AND WEEPING JAPANESE MAPLE, this small pond cretes an unexpected yet serene spot in the garden. A seemingly random combination of boulders, liriope, and ferns create an irregular, natural-looking edge around the water.

◄ PONDS PLACED NEAR architectural spaces such as this patio are often less naturalistic than ponds found in the landscape because they serve in a transitional role. This raised pond is clearly man-made, but the stones provide a strong visual link to the surrounding landscape.

▼ NEATNESS DOESN'T NECESSARILY count when it comes to creating a naturalistic setting. In fact, it's the dark pond bottom, irregularly placed boulders, sprawling ferns, and leaf litter that make this man-made pond look convincingly natural.

◄ ▲ ALTHOUGH THIS POND HAS BEEN positioned as a garden destination along the woodland edge, it receives enough sunlight (four to six hours a day) for a few water lilies and irises to grow. Moisture- and shade-loving perennials offer an ever-changing show along the pond's edge. Primroses bloom in early spring, followed by astilbes in summer. Ferns offer leafy texture all season long and moss grows easily on the damp, shaded rocks that surround the water.

► MOST WATER PLANTS prefer sun, but these caladiums thrive in the shade. The bulbs were planted right at the pond's edge so that their bold white leaves would be reflected in the water—brightening a shady corner of the garden.

The Bottom Line on Gravel

POND BUILDERS CONTINUE THE DEBATE over whether or not to cover the bottom of a pond with gravel. For ponds with bottom drains, a layer of gravel can help filter the water. Plus gravel hides the liner in a new pool. Because debris settles and algae grow on the bottom of a pond, gravel makes pond cleanup more challenging. However, stone is an expensive element in pond building, and after a few weeks, it's rare that the bottom of a pond is even visible. So unless you have a bottom drain or dislike the look of your pond liner, gravel is probably an unnecessary expense.

▼ THE DARKER THE POND, the better the reflections. Of course, it's not the water but the liner and sediment that make it dark. This raised pond is located in the front yard of a Florida-style cottage garden where it reflects bold foliage and bright sunshine.

▲ A FRONT YARD IS A WONDERFUL PLACE for a small fish pond. These homeowners enjoy sitting on their front porch on comfortable evenings watching the koi; arriving guests are entertained by the koi's antics while waiting at the front door.

◀ ▲ ALTHOUGH THIS CITY
garden has been in development
for 20 years, the pond was rebuilt
just months before this photo
was taken. With approximately
400 square feet of surface area,
it provides a home for numerous
koi. Since koi are notorious for
destroying water plants, all of
the plantings are placed around,
rather than within, the pond.
Ornamental grasses, rushes,
ferns, fragrant herbs, and bold-
foliaged plants such as ligularia
are the workhorses in this textural garden.

The Flexibility of Pond Liners

PREFORMED PONDS AND CONCRETE PONDS have their place in pond building, but liners made from synthetic rubber offer the greatest design flexibility, are generally the easiest to install, and should last 20 to 30 years. The key to longevity is buying a thick (30 to 45 mil), high-quality EPDM liner specified for pond use and using two layers of underlayment—one on the bottom and another on top—to protect the liner. Avoid substituting carpet for commercially available underlayment, as it may void the manufacturer's warranty on the liner, will deteriorate, and can attract termites. Pond liners can also be used for streams and waterfalls.

◄ THESE HOMEOWNERS each have basement studios that overlook the pond, and the small bluestone deck provides a quiet, contemplative spot for breaks during the work day as well as a place to enjoy their morning coffee.

▲ THE MOST IMPORTANT factor to consider when placing a pond is visibility. This large pond (actually one of two connected, man-made garden ponds) is easily viewed from the house, porch, garden, and surrounding landscape. Open to the sky, it provides an ever-changing parade of reflections.

◄ EXPOSED ON ONE SIDE, this pond offers a nice mix of sun and shade that makes it suitable for fish. With small ornamental trees on the southwest side, it receives morning light but is screened from the hotter afternoon sun.

▲ THIS KOI POND FEATURES a small waterfall that both filters the water and provides a pleasant gurgling sound in an in-town neighborhood. It was built adjacent to the house so that it could be seen and heard from the breakfast room that overlooks the garden.

▲ WHEN THIS STILL POND WAS BUILT, all the leaves from the site were bagged and then spread back out after construction was complete. The result is a pond that looks like it has been there for many years.

Fish

Fish add life, color, and motion to ponds. They also feast on mosquito larvae and string algae while fertilizing plants. Most fish prefer shade, and floating plants and stone ledges provide cool hiding places for fish.

Goldfish are the easiest to keep. They grow to 16 inches and often live for 12 years. Varieties include the common goldfish, comet, shubunkin, fantail, veiltail, and moor. Goldfish can flourish in as little as 18 inches of water and require little, if any, supplemental feeding. They nibble on plants rather than devour them, making them a good choice for water gardens. Filtration systems are rarely necessary, but aeration is important when hot weather reduces oxygen levels in the water.

Koi grow up to 3 feet and 45 pounds, with life spans exceeding 50 years. The many varieties—from Asagi and Bekko to Sanke and Utsuri—are classified by color, pattern, and scale type. Koi require considerable space—at least 100 gallons of water per fish (this translates into a pond approximately 7 feet wide by 8 feet long by 4 feet deep). Ponds should be at least 2 feet deep in mild climates and 4 feet deep in colder climates for winter survival, and a filtration system is required. Koi damage plants, so they're not the best choice for water gardens.

Mosquito fish are ideal for small water gardens, golden orfe make good companions for goldfish and koi, and rainbow darters are suitable for moving water.

▲ SHALLOW SHELVES WERE CREATED along this pond's edge, where marginal perennials such as 'Yellow Flag' iris, ferns, and sweet flag could grow. Water lilies, which prefer deeper water, were submerged in pots on the pond's bottom.

Ducks

Wood ducks and Mandarin ducks—which are smaller and quieter than most other ducks—are ideal for backyard ponds and can provide hours of entertainment. Because they require considerable care and feeding, they should be considered pets rather than wildlife.

If you're considering ducks, start with a single pair and make sure you understand the commitment you are making. You'll want to clip young ducklings' wings to keep them from flying off into the neighbor's yard or beyond, and enclose an area to help keep predators such as cats, opossums, and hawks at bay (be sure to cover the top and sides). A 3-foot-deep pond will encourage ducks to dive and play, while an island will provide a daytime haven. Consider a sandy or grassy beach leading into the pond so ducks have a place to preen. Winter protection in cold climates may also be necessary.

Keeping the pond clean is the greatest challenge for duck owners, as ducks create considerable waste. This litters the pond edge and increases nitrogen levels that encourage algae growth in the pond. Algaecides, water plants, and a regular inflow of water will help keep the pond fresh. Ducks may eat water lilies, water hyacinths, and small koi, so avoid them.

▲ Mallards

◄ THESE BOULDERS WERE RESCUED from a site destined for development. Before they were moved, the landscape contractor noted the light conditions at the original location and matched them as closely as possible at the new pond site so that the moss and fungi would continue to grow.

► WATER GARDENS, just like perennial beds or mixed borders, benefit from a strong color scheme. The yellow foliage of golden hops, hakone grass, and golden sedge, along with the yellow flowers of lady's mantle and spurge, create a powerful sense of unity in this small garden.

◄ A SMALL POND JUST INSIDE the entry courtyard garden in this Pacific Northwest garden makes it a destination as well as a transitional area. Strategically placed, upright boulders along the pond edge help carry out the Japanese garden theme established by the arbor and fence details.

▲ ALTHOUGH THE LOTUS, HOSTA, IRIS, SEDUM, and lady's mantle surrounding this pond all sport flowers
at their designated times, their striking foliage makes for a good-looking setting all season long.

◀ GROTTOS, or cave-like dwellings with water, have a rich history dating back to Greek and Italian Renaissance gardens. The dense, lush plantings and architectural "ruins" create an intriguing grotto-like setting in this California garden.

▼ A THIN LAYER of open-weave, black netting is nearly invisible and keeps both leaves and wildlife out of the pond. Plastic netting won't rust or contaminate the water, and can easily be secured with stones or anchor pins.

ON THE WILD SIDE

Keeping Critters Out

One of best things about a pond is the wildlife it attracts. But when a pond includes fish, unwanted guests may show up, too. Herons, raccoons, and cats, in particular, are notorious for seeking out garden ponds and dining on their inhabitants. The best way to protect fish is to give them plenty of places to hide beneath plants or overhanging rocks. Building at least part of your pond more than 2 feet deep will help put them out of reach of predators as well. If all else fails, consider covering the pond with woven deer fencing or building an attractive bamboo barrier.

Streams and Waterfalls

STREAMS AND WATERFALLS ANIMATE A POND. Not only do they provide music to the ears, but that sound serves as a magnet for wildlife as well. Moving water helps aerate a pond and keep down mosquito larvae, while the rocks and mechanical filters help cleanse the water of debris.

The water's point of origin as well as the edges of the stream or waterfall should be concealed with stones or plants so that it appears to flow from a natural source. Water tends to wend its way downhill, so seek a sloped location and lay out a meandering path for the streambed. Lay a waterfall's boulders in such a way that water moves asymmetrically over the rocks—utilizing the entire width of the waterfall—to keep it natural looking as well as to balance the water flow. Limiting the stone used to one type and varying its shape and size will give water features a more natural appearance.

▲ THE FULL WIDTH OF A WATERFALL should be utilized, with water zigzagging back and forth as it works its way toward the pond. Sealing the stones with expanding foam (available in cans from home centers) ensures that water flows over the rocks rather than between the rocks and liner.

▶ SMALL WATERFALLS can be constructed in almost any setting, as evidenced by this enclosed southwestern backyard. Although the site is flat, installing raised planting beds allowed a waterfall to be created, providing dimension and texture to the area. The waterfall adds height, movement, and sound.

▲ NATURALISTIC PLANTINGS TAKE THEIR CUES FROM NATURE—but they don't necessarily
copy it. The plantings around this waterfall are grown in natural-looking layers, yet foliage colors,
leaf shapes, and growth habits are carefully orchestrated for a neat, trim appearance.

▲ THIS WATERFALL AND KOI POND combine natural and faux boulders—although it is extremely difficult to tell them apart. (Hint: The large boulder in the top right corner was carved from concrete and stained.)

▶ THIS NATURAL-LOOKING STREAM started its life as an ordinary drainage ditch. During rainstorms, it still carries runoff to a lake at the bottom of the hill. In dry weather, water is pumped uphill from the lake so that water continuously runs downstream.

NUTS AND BOLTS

Designing a Waterfall

The first step in designing a waterfall is determining its location. In most cases, a spot roughly opposite the primary viewing area (typically a house or patio) with the water falling toward it is best. The height and width of a waterfall are also important, as they should be in scale with both the pond and the surrounding landscape. Large waterfalls can overwhelm a small backyard, just as tiny waterfalls can look lost in a larger property. For the most naturalistic look, waterfalls should relate to the surrounding terrain: flat lots look best with subtle waterfalls, while rugged terrain can support a taller drop.

When installing your waterfall, cluster boulders randomly and bury them by at least one-third. Using a single type of stone will result in a more natural look. The waterfall box, which contains a biological filter (which traps solid matter and toxic wastes) and spillway, should be concealed (along with the GFCI outlet) with stones and plants, and the skimmer (which removes floating debris as water exits the pond) should be placed roughly opposite the waterfall.

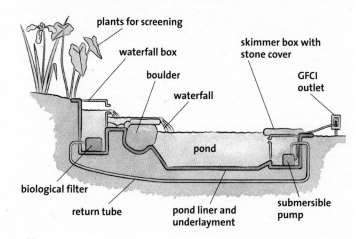

plants for screening
waterfall box
boulder
waterfall
skimmer box with stone cover
GFCI outlet
pond
biological filter
return tube
pond liner and underlayment
submersible pump

Turtles

Turtles do best in garden ponds when they have an area designed specifically for them. Otherwise, they tend to tear through pond liners with their claws. A preformed pond unit and the heaviest flexible pond liner available are both good choices.

Although some types of turtles enjoy deep water, shallow water and broad water surfaces best suit most turtles. Several areas at different depths with sloping terrain between them are ideal. Be sure to include logs, rocks, or planks so the turtles can bask in the sun and a bit of dry land (perhaps an island) where they can ramble about. Hiding areas both in and out of the water are also important—broad plant leaves or cantilevered rocks will do the trick—to help keep them from predators. Although turtles will damage plants over time, floating and marginal plants such as water lettuce, anarchis, tape grass, rushes, and cattails will help provide shelter and shade, as well as nourishment.

▲ ROCKS CAREFULLY CONCEAL THE WATERFALL BOX through which this pond's recirculated water is funneled and filtered. A skimmer box on the opposite side of the pond culls leaves, acorns, and other debris from the water's surface and routes water back to the waterfall.

▲ Western painted turtle

▶ DENSE PLANTINGS ALONG THE EDGE of this stream make it all the more unexpected. The stream runs parallel to a path that leads to the home's front door, creating a unique and relaxing welcome for guests.

◄ ▲ THESE FOUR STONES WERE CAREFULLY reassembled as they were found in nature (where, over time, they had divided from a single stone) to create a hybrid fountain and pondless waterfall. Positioned at the corner of a flagstone terrace, it can be seen from the house and heard while relaxing or dining outdoors. The water vanishes beneath river cobbles into an underground basin for recirculation.

▲ THIS PINT-SIZED POND AND
WATERFALL were built into a
berm, or raised bed of earth,
that helps provide privacy screening in a very shallow backyard.
The trickling water helps create
a soothing atmosphere for the
homeowners, who enjoy dining
on the adjacent patio.

◀ THE GRADE OF THIS streambed changes as it meanders
downhill, with occasional short
drops to add visual interest.
Rocks of different sizes are
combined in random, yet con-
sciously controlled, ways that
help establish the speed and
direction of water flow.

▲ A BUBBLING STONE provides a mysterious and compelling source of water for this pond. To create this effect, a hole was drilled through the stone with a long masonry bit. A small tube was then run from the pump through the stone.

▲ THESE BOULDERS WERE CAREFULLY LAID to replicate the natural strata of stones found in nearby mountain streams. Boulders are buried by one-third or more, and bagged leaves were spread up to their edges, making this stream and waterfall look as if it were designed by Mother Nature herself just weeks after it was created.

Marginals

Marginal plants are those that reside along the edge of a pond or in shallow water where they create a habitat for many amphibians and insects. They thrive in soggy soils and don't mind having their roots covered with water, yet can tolerate occasional periods where the soil dries out completely. In man-made water features, these plants can be grown in pots that are set in shallow water or planted directly in specially created bogs along the edge of the pond. A few good marginal plants include:

Arrowhead	(*Sagittaria* spp.)
Bog arum	(*Calla palustris*)
Bowles golden sedge	(*Carex elata* 'Aurea')
Cardinal flower	(*Lobelia cardinalis*)
Daylily	(*Hemerocallis* hybrids)
Great bulrush	(*Schoenoplectus tabernaemontani*)
Hardy water canna	(*Thalia dealbata*)
Iris	(*Iris laevigata, I. versicolor, I. ensata*)
Lizard's tail	(*Saururus cernuus*)
Marsh marigold	(*Caltha palustris*)
Pickerelweed	(*Pontederia cordata*)
Rush	(*Juncus effusius*)
Sweet flag	(*Acorus calamus*)
Watercress	(*Nasturtium officinale*)

▲ Pickerelweed

▶ THESE CANDELABRA-TYPE PRIMROSES are an excellent choice for naturally occurring streams, ephemeral ponds, and in the moist bogs of man-made ponds. There are dozens of varieties to choose from that bloom beginning in late winter or early spring.

▲ THIS SMALL WATERFALL sits along the edge of a small patio, just steps away from an outdoor kitchen and dining area. Both the patio and fountain have been illuminated, creating a romantic setting to watch the sun set over southern New Mexico's Organ Mountains.

Visualizing the Flow of Water

DECIDING HOW THE WATER SHOULD FALL OVER ROCKS is an art that benefits from the careful observation of mountain rivers, streams, and waterfalls. Only rarely does water flow in a single stream or in the middle of a river. Instead, it tumbles and falls in a random, asymmetric manner utilizing the entire width of the water course. It may drop airborne to a pool below or form a fast-moving sluice as it glides over smooth rocks. The shape and size of individual rocks, as well as their placement in relationship to other rocks, will determine where the water flows. In a man-made waterfall, this takes some experimenting. Use a garden hose to see how the water flows over stones, and move rocks around until the results are pleasing.

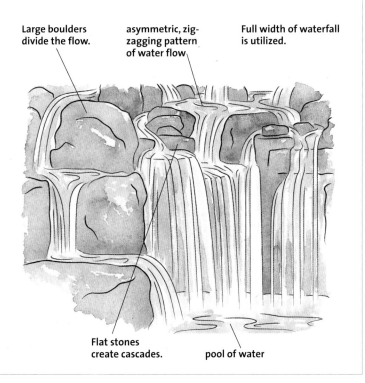

Large boulders divide the flow.

asymmetric, zig-zagging pattern of water flow

Full width of waterfall is utilized.

Flat stones create cascades.

pool of water

▶ TWO CONNECTED PONDS can be more interesting than one. A recirculating pump pulls water from the lower pond back to the upper pond. The lower pond is large enough to hold all overflow water from the upper pool when the pump is turned off.

▼ THE GENTLE FLOW OF WATER from beneath these moss-covered stones implies a spring as the source of water. In reality, it's simply water recirculating from the pond, but by camouflaging the actual water source, the mind is allowed to draw more natural conclusions.

▶ BEAUTIFUL CASCADES CAN BE CREATED by allowing water to flow over a large flat rock that extends beyond the stream wall. The bottom stone causes the water to spread horizontally across the surface of the water in a unique fanlike pattern.

▼ STREAMS DON'T NEED TO DROP MUCH— 2 inches every 10 feet to 15 feet is sufficient to propel water downstream. They can either flow steadily like this one or form a series of flat sections followed by short drops.

▶ A WATERFALL CONSISTING OF SEVERAL cascades was built into the stacked-stone retaining wall above this pond. The stream disappears around a bend uphill beyond the flowering dogwood tree, subtly concealing its origin and creating a sense of intrigue.

◀ THE GENTLE CURVE OF THIS GARDEN stream is pleasing to the eye because it's so natural. Several flat stones have been laid in the streambed to create a series of small cascades for added interest as the water makes its way downstream.

Playing with Boulder Placement

WHEN LAYING OUT A RECIRCU-LATING STREAM, dry stream-bed, waterfall, or even a pond, try this trick: fill trash bags with different amounts of leaves and tie them shut. Then place the bags (now different sizes) where similarly sized boulders might go. Keep moving the bags around, trying the "boulders" individually and in groups—clusters of three or five work especially well—until the composition is appealing. When it's time to set the real stones, start with the largest boulders, then move to the midsized rocks, and finish off with the smaller river cobbles.

▼ THESE BOULDERS WERE PHOTOGRAPHED and marked before they were moved from a site slated for demolition. This assisted the landscape contractor in placing them in a backyard waterfall so that their strata aligns naturally. The separation between the lower boulders occurred naturally many years ago.

▲ STONES AND PLANTS WORK TOGETHER to conceal the artificial edges and waterproof barrier of this recirculating garden stream. Gravelly soil has been placed on top of the liner along the water's edge to create planting pockets among the rocks where marginal plants can be grown without their pots.

► THIS TRICKLING WATERFALL is actually a bog-style filter for a large pond. The raised area was filled with rough gravel, topped with decorative pea gravel, and planted. Water from the pond filters through the bog as it is being recirculated.

▼ PONDS AND WATERFALLS CAN SUIT even the smallest of garden spaces. In this walled garden, water trickles rather than cascades over the rocks, creating the perfect conditions for moss to grow. A small submersible pump suitable for container fountains produces just enough water flow for this effect.

▼ PONDLESS WATERFALLS AND STREAMS, like this one that trickles down a hillside, are intriguing in their own right because the water vanishes mysteriously into the ground. But they're also good choices when space or budgets don't permit the construction of a pond, or for safety if there are young children around.

▲ DESPITE ITS RELATIVELY SMALL SIZE, this waterfall creates a sense of drama in a Japanese garden as a significant volume of water is forced through a narrow slot, then falls nearly a foot, splashing into a dark pool of water.

▲ THE SOUND OF WATER IS DETERMINED primarily by the volume of water, the distance it falls, and the surface onto which it falls. Here, a subtle trickling sound is created by a little bit of water falling a modest distance onto pebbles.

▲ WATERFALLS SHOULD BE DESIGNED IN SCALE with the accompanying pond. A broad or tall waterfall, for instance, would look entirely out of place with this small pond. This waterfall is just large enough to draw your attention and create a picturesque setting.

DRY STREAMS

▶ THIS STREAMBED MEANDERS GENTLY through the woods, working its way around trees in a natural way. The streambed is set on a gentle slope and recessed slightly below ground level both to catch rainfall and appear naturally weather worn.

▲ PLANTS ARE JUST AS IMPORTANT along a streambed as they are around a pond. This stream ducks almost mysteriously in and out of the colorful Arkansas blue star and ornamental grasses. Plants chosen for a dry stream should tolerate occasional "wet feet."

▶ THE VARIED SIZE AND COLOR and random placement of stones in this streambed creates an engaging
design. The smallest cobbles weigh just enough that
they won't be washed downstream in a storm, and a few
plants growing among the cobbles help slow and filter
the running water.

◀ ▼ ALTHOUGH THE BOULDERS are much bigger in the shady, steeply sloped
backyard than the sunny, gently sloped front yard, the river cobbles create a sense
of continuity as this dry streambed flows through the property. The homeowners
nixed the builder's recommendation for a large concrete swale, turning instead to
a streambed to carry the heavy runoff from neighboring properties in this urban
Atlanta subdivision.

Designing a Streambed

Both streams that always have water and dry streambeds that fill only after a good rain wend their way along, often widening at bends and then narrowing again as they go. If you'll be building a garden stream on a hillside or one that needs to handle considerable water volume, place large boulders at these bends to slow and redirect the water. Fill in with mid-sized rocks and cover the bottom of the streambed with cobbles. The smallest cobbles should be large enough that they won't be washed downhill in a strong storm.

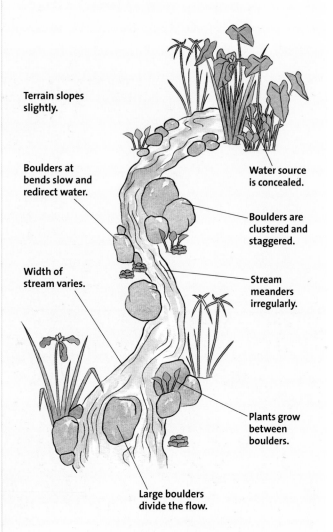

Terrain slopes slightly.

Boulders at bends slow and redirect water.

Width of stream varies.

Water source is concealed.

Boulders are clustered and staggered.

Stream meanders irregularly.

Plants grow between boulders.

Large boulders divide the flow.

▲ IN A SEASONALLY DRY CLIMATE like northern California, this streambed helps call attention to rainwater when it falls. Even in the dry season, a streambed helps the garden feel just a little bit cooler by conjuring up an image of water.

▶ IN THE DESERT SOUTHWEST, this dry stream rarely sees rushes of water, but it greatly enhances the xeric landscape. When the rains do come, the dry stream helps channel the runoff into a dry well where it can slowly seep into the soil.

▼ DESIGNED SPECIFICALLY TO CHANNEL rainwater runoff away from the driveway and garden, this dry stream is filled with river cobbles and anchored with firmly rooted plants that help slow the flow of water. This prevents erosion and encourages water to soak into the ground.

▲ THIS DRY STREAM turned an eyesore into an appealing woodland garden feature. A 24-inch storm drain dumps water from neighboring properties into the streambed during heavy rains, so the stones also help control what had become a significant erosion problem.

At the Water's Edge

WHILE PONDS CAN BE ENJOYED FROM A DISTANCE, up close they reveal colorful reflections, the sound of songbirds, the plopping of bullfrogs into the water, the subtle textures of plantings, and the mesmerizing movement of fish. Including a small sitting area near the pond—whether a gravel patio, screened gazebo, Japanese tea house, or even a small dock—will ensure that the water garden will be a favorite gathering place in the landscape. Crossing over water is another experience that can be enjoyed in a backyard garden. Placing rustic footbridges, decorative bridges, or even simple but sturdy utility bridges across streams or along the water's edge is a great way to get up close and personal with plants and critters that live in and around the water. These structures can have low profiles that simply provide access to the water or rise above the water level as focal points in the landscape.

▲ THIS WOODEN DOCK was built on piers over a large garden pond, providing a place to launch a canoe or gather with friends. Seating is built into the railings and wisteria hangs from the arbor overhead. There's enough room even for a small dinner party.

◄ MARGINAL PLANTS GROW DENSELY along the stream bank and all the way up to the base of this handcrafted iron bridge. The decorative railing makes the bridge a focal point and destination, as well as a functional structure in the landscape.

▲ A CASUAL SEATING AREA just above this small waterfall serves as a relaxing destination as the sun falls below the horizon. Candlelight, the gurgling stream, and the splashing waterfall (which spills into a swimming pool) help create a romantic setting.

◄ THE SIMPLEST DESIGNS are often the most effective. This plank boardwalk settles easily into the landscape, calling attention to the pond rather than to itself. Such narrow passageways that wend their way across a pond can be more intriguing than broad, straight bridges.

▲ THIS CURVED BRIDGE lends a storybook quality
to the watery landscape, bringing to mind images of
Monet's garden in Giverny, France. This one is simply
designed, with a low arch and single railing, allowing
the colorful perennials to take center stage.

▶ BEYOND WHITE, red is the most dominant color
in the landscape and should be used with intention.
Here, an elegantly designed red bridge calls attention
to the stream, flowering trees, and shrubs—beckoning garden visitors to explore the trails through the
woods beyond.

Designing a Bog Garden

Bogs are areas of soil that remain damp year-round, making them suitable for either bog or marginal plants. An artificial bog can be easily created adjacent to a garden pond by digging a 12-inch to 18-inch depression that is covered with the pool liner and filled with a mix of friable soil and fine gravel. Place a dry-stacked stone barrier fitted with mesh between the pond and bog to allow water to seep into the bog but prevent bog soil from spilling into the pond. Remove plants from their containers and plant them directly in the bog.

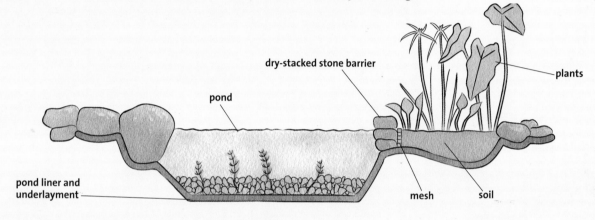

dry-stacked stone barrier

plants

pond

pond liner and underlayment

mesh

soil

◄ WHEN STREAMS CROSS A LANDSCAPE, a bridge plays an important role in providing access to the other side for both pleasure and maintenance. Short and sturdy, this bridge is wide enough to accommodate a push mower or garden cart filled with tools or mulch.

▶ EXTENDING THE CANTILEVERED blue-stone paving slightly over the water's edge creates the illusion that the pond is larger than it really is. It also provides a sitting area close to the water where one can quietly observe the fish, bullfrogs, and dragonflies.

▼ ALTHOUGH JUST ABOUT ANY materials can be used for a pondside sitting area, wood planks immediately bring to mind a dock—whether or not it is floating on the water. Low, dense plantings help make this one a cozy spot for enjoying the water view.

▲ THE POTTING SHED both has a view and creates a view—adding a strong vertical accent above the broad horizontal plane of the pond. A small deck extends over the water, providing a visual connection between the potting shed and the pond.

◄ ONE HOMEOWNER CALLS THIS a "water temple." The other jokingly refers to it as the "water closet." Either way, it's simply a folly to add interest to a backyard waterscape. Recirculated water flows out from the structure, down a small stream, and into a pond.

Bog Plants

Bog plants, like marginal plants, are often seen in sunny, moist, low-lying areas just beyond a pond's edge. Unlike marginals, however, bog plants do not like their roots to be submerged in standing water and suffer if the soil dries out completely. Plants that thrive in bog conditions include:

American pitcher plant	(*Sarracenia* spp.)
Bog gentian	(*Gentiana catesbaei*)
Grass pink	(*Calopogon* spp.)
False spirea	(*Astilbe* spp.)
Orange milkwort	(*Polygala lutea*)
Primrose	(*Primula* spp.)
Swamp milkweed	(*Asclepias incarnata*)
Sundew	(*Drosera* spp.)
Venus flytrap	(*Dionaea muscipula*)
Umbrella plant	(*Darmera peltata*)

▲ Ligularia and astilbe

◀ Cardinal flower and variegated sweet flag

◄ THIS RAISED PATIO IS A DESTINATION in the landscape, providing comfortable seating in a secluded area overlooking the pond and a small waterfall. Ivy scrambles around its base, creating an evergreen skirt to hide its pilings.

▼ SECURELY ANCHORED STEPPING-STONES provide access for the curious from a small dock to an unseen, yet beckoning garden beyond. Bright-green water lettuce fills in around the stones, creating strong visual contrast on the water's surface.

▲ ALL PATHS LEAD to this pond, which lies at the heart of the garden. A built-in stone bench doubles as a retaining wall and provides a quiet place to pause when working on garden chores or touring the garden. A star magnolia blooming in the foreground helps to frame the view.

◄ THIS LARGE, FLAT BOULDER looks right at home. With water flowing beneath the stone rather than over it, a natural bridge is created over the dry stream. Smaller boulders help anchor the large stone and make a gradual visual transition to the smaller cobbles.

Invasive Aquatic Plants

MANY COMMON AQUATIC PLANTS that are well-behaved in some states are classified as "invasive" in other states where conditions allow them to spread rapidly without natural controls (often by seed-carrying birds), out-competing more desirable plants and often reducing food sources or habitats for birds and other animals. Before acquiring plants for a water garden, research your state's invasive plant list (most are available online). You may be surprised to find plants such as purple loosestrife, water hyacinth, yellow flag iris, hydrilla, milfoil, water lettuce, parrot's feather, and cattails on the list.

▶ NATURALISTIC SETTINGS call for natural elements. Here, boards cut lengthwise from a locust tree, which is a rot-resistant wood, make a footbridge that blends almost seamlessly into the landscape.

◀ THIS RUSTIC PARK-STYLE BENCH was built with 2x4s laid on edge and positioned above copper support posts. The clean, simple design suits the serene atmosphere of the water garden and allows the more colorful irises and primroses to take center stage.

▶ THIS SLIGHTLY ARCHED BRIDGE is just wide enough for shuttling mowers and gardening equipment across a stone-lined drainage channel. The design, which features 1x4s tacked to three 2x6 support braces cut in the shape of an arch, is simple enough that it can be tackled by most DIYers.

◀ WHILE THIS POND IS TOO SMALL FOR A CANOE, it still benefits from a small dock that extends 5 feet over the water. It adds dimension to the pond and provides a spot to sit and dangle your legs in the water.

▲ THIS SMALL STONE BRIDGE that spans a dry stream in a woodland garden was modeled after a sketch from a book on medieval technology. It was built with a plywood template, concrete, and stone.

▲ A SERIES OF FOCAL POINTS—a spouting stone, heron statuary, and a bridge—visually draw you through this water garden to the ultimate destination, a Japanese-style tea house. It's the perfect spot for contemplation or a cup of tea.

▲ THIS ARCHED BRIDGE crosses nearly 4 feet above a dry stream that leads from the house to a vegetable garden, so hardware cloth was tacked to the railing as a safety measure. The large mesh is sturdy but still allows the garden to be seen.

◄ WATERSIDE SEATING doesn't have to be elaborate, expensive, or even store-bought. A tree stump serves admirably beside this small fish and frog pond, creating a casual resting spot in a small backyard.

► EVEN THOUGH WOODEN BRIDGES can blend with their surroundings, sometimes they would be out of place. This stone "bridge" continues the stone path and is secured to support stones with concrete so they don't rock when stepped on.

A Floating Island Planter

Floating island planters are an excellent way to introduce plants for shade and cover to ponds while protecting them from grazing koi. These floating containers come in a variety of sizes and styles and can be anchored to the pond's edge or allowed to float freely in the pond. Most are self-watering, making them easy to care for and ideal for marsh and bog plants, including carnivorous pitcher plants. Plant them as you would other containers—creating favorite color and texture combinations with multiple plants. Try a spiky plant in the center, trailing plants along the edges, and clumping filler plants in between. Just be sure the plants you choose like having wet feet.

▲ Carnivorous pitcher plants in a floating island planter

▲ LARGE PONDS CAN ACCOMMODATE LARGE DOCKS. This one extends about 15 feet and is just wide enough for a few folding chairs. Cottonwoods surrounding the pond cast a golden glow at sunrise, making the dock a magical place for a morning cup of joe.

Architectural Waterworks

ARCHITECTURAL WATER FEATURES—those that are built rather than bought and geometric rather than naturalistic in design—are often dominant elements in the landscape, especially when accompanied by underwater or landscape lighting for dramatic effects after dark. The features themselves—not plants—are the focal point. And while many draw their inspiration from the formal European fountains and watercourses of past centuries, others are inspired by modern materials and contemporary styles.

Architectural waterworks tend to relate more closely to a home's architecture than to the surrounding landscape, though their role is often to bridge the gap between the two. These types of water features include large fountains, wall fountains, cascades, and watercourses, which may be built from concrete, stone, tile, brick, or modern materials such as glass bricks or metal. Whether symmetric or asymmetric, architectural waterworks are most often composed of regular shapes such as squares, rectangles, circles, or ovals. Architects and landscape architects frequently design them, while contractors and design/build firms construct them. Special building permits are often required.

◄ STILL PONDS PROVIDE THE BEST REFLECTIONS, especially if they have dark bottoms. This one reflects the evening sky, as well as the swordlike foliage of water plants, and was positioned within easy viewing distance of the porch.

Large Pools and Fountains

POOLS WITH FOUNTAINS are the most traditional and time-tested of all man-made water features. A subtle addition to the landscape, in-ground pools allow other elements to dominate the view, while above-ground pools and basins, especially if equipped with fountains, tend to break up distant views and dominate the landscape.

Raised pools and fountains are often built at sitting height, making them a favorite destination. In-ground reflecting pools surrounded by a sea of lawn or paving are often best viewed at a distance or from an elevated position.

Since many larger fountains take their cues from classic water features, they are most commonly built in formal shapes such as circles, ovals, and octagons—especially when placed in a central location. Rectangular or L-shaped pools are ideally suited to the edge of a patio or against a wall, and can be easily fitted with multiple fountain heads for a dramatic effect.

▲ THE WALLS SURROUNDING this traditional wall fountain enhance the sound of falling water, while the fountain transforms what is often dead space at the bottom of a stairwell into a compelling outdoor room. The stone creates a sense of unity between the house and landscaping.

▼ THIS L-SHAPED FOUNTAIN anchors the corner of a patio, helping to define an outdoor room. Materials have been carefully coordinated, with the same stone used for the fountain and as an accent in the paving. At 15 inches high, the wall provides extra seating.

▲ CREATIVE USE OF MATERIALS makes this simple rectangular pool more interesting. River cobbles embedded among the flag-stone vary its texture, pattern, and color. Instead of a spouting pipe or fountainhead, water spurts through a smooth river stone.

▶ THIS LONG, NARROW reflecting pool feels more like a channel. It was built at sitting height and serves as a low wall dividing a large space into a series of more intimate outdoor rooms. Fences and gates also help frame these spaces.

▼ BY APPROACHING WATER PLANTS as part of the garden's overall planting design (rather than designing the pond plantings separately), this raised pool blends in almost seamlessly. The consistent use of stone on the patio, raised pool, and garden also helps to create a sense of unity.

▼ WITH A LITTLE INGENUITY, concrete, and a wooden form, fountains can be designed in just about any shape to create a one-of-a-kind water feature. Raised above the pool level for increased visibility, this colorful, six-pointed star is covered in decorative glazed tile. A return pipe and fountainhead are embedded in the concrete.

◄ ▲ THREE TYPES OF LIGHTING were combined to create this romantic outdoor setting. Strings of tea lights attached to the arbor provide general illumination. A downlight calls attention to the bubbling granite fountain. Submersible lights add a mysterious glow in the basin beneath the fountain.

▲ A CIRCLE, the most formal shape in any landscape, forms an appropriate water feature in this formal boxwood garden. The uniformly massed annuals surrounding the fountain, as well as the statuary and crown spray pattern blend appropriately into the setting.

▶ THE CONCENTRIC ARRANGEMENT of granite cobbles and the continuous flow of water from the end of each rill to the center well was conceived to convey the impression of more water than is actually present. For the owner, the three rills represent longevity, vitality, and radiant health.

▼ ▶ BRIGHTLY PAINTED STUCCO WALLS and a blue-stone cap make this rectangular pool a distinctive design element in a small northern California backyard. In an intentional juxtaposition, the pool is filled with water-loving plants but is surrounded by a dramatic collection of succulents, which thrive in arid conditions. They have been planted in a well-drained, gravelly soil mix.

◄ THIS RAISED FOUNTAIN features
five stainless-steel jets. Their spouting height can be raised for a more
dramatic sight and sound, or lowered
to minimize the sound and spray. The
upright stones around the base add a
vertical element to the broad patio.

► TO KEEP MAINTENANCE to a
minimum, it's usually better to
place water features away from
deciduous trees. Admittedly,
these cottonwood leaves will
eventually have to be cleared
from the fountain, but for now,
they add an element of design
and delight to this landscape.

Water Lilies

Water lilies are perhaps the most popular of all water plants. There are two groups of water lilies: hardy and tropical. Hardy water lilies are mostly day-blooming plants that bear floating flowers and leaves, and that can be left to grow outdoors. Tropical water lilies can be day- or night-blooming, generally display larger flowers than hardy water lilies, and tend to hold their flowers on stems above the water. However, they must be lifted from the water garden after a few hard frosts, overwintered indoors, and replanted in the spring. Regardless of which group you choose, plant water lilies in pots to contain their roots and then submerge the pots so that the top of the pot is 6 inches to 10 inches under water.

Local and mail-order nurseries specializing in aquatic plants usually offer dozens of varieties of water lilies. Here are a few worth checking out:

Nymphaea 'Antares'	tropical, night-blooming, red
Nymphaea 'Attraction'	hardy, day-blooming, red
Nymphaea 'Blue Beauty'	tropical, day-blooming, blue
Nymphaea 'Charlene Strawn'	hardy, day-blooming, yellow
Nymphaea 'Chromatella'	hardy, day-blooming, yellow
Nymphaea 'Denver'	hardy, day-blooming, white
Nymphaea 'Georgia Peach'	hardy, day-blooming, peach
Nymphaea 'Helvola'	hardy, day-blooming, red
Nymphaea 'Hollandia'	hardy, day-blooming, pink
Nymphaea 'Rose Arey'	hardy, day-blooming, pink
Nymphaea 'Trudy Slocum'	tropical, day-blooming, white
Victoria cruziana	tropical, night-blooming, white to pink

▲ PAVING WAS LAID AT AN ANGLE to the raised pool and tiered fountain to create an element of tension that adds excitement to this small, Pacific Northwest backyard. Planting pockets created in both the patio flooring and the pool allow bursts of color and texture all around this backyard focal point.

'Shirley Byrne' tropical, day-blooming water lily

Giant pads of the Santa Cruz water lily

◀ ▲ DESIGNED AS A CHILD'S PLAY SPACE, this concrete patio features a tile mosaic spiral that ends in a water spout. The spiral is just the right size for a small tricycle track, while the spout offers kids of all sizes an opportunity to cool off in warm weather.

▲ ILLUMINATED HAND-BLOWN
glass orbs can add drama to any
water feature, whether they're
in the water or placed in the area
surrounding it. This one glows like
a ball of fire, casting a soft light
on nearby water plants.

◄ THE SIMPLEST DESIGNS often
yield the most soothing settings. This round, shallow pool
and trickling statuary fountain
is set in a small side-yard lawn.
The simply designed teak chair
enhances the composition and offers a quiet respite from backyard
activities.

▲ THIS SCULPTURAL WALL FOUNTAIN is a great example of a water feature that was inspired by its setting. The organic colors mimic those found in the mountains of the desert Southwest, which have been framed by a narrow opening in the courtyard wall, while the clean lines, simple materials, and minimalist plantings complement the setting.

Raised Pools

Raised pools are relatively easy to construct since they can be formed with concrete block set on a reinforced concrete foundation, and then finished in brick, stone, tile, or stucco. They also may be built entirely from reinforced concrete and then finished with stucco, though this might not be something the average DIYer can tackle. Regardless of the construction method and finish, the interior must be either coated with a waterproof sealer or constructed with a flexible pond liner that is secured beneath the capstone with waterproof caulking. In addition to the beauty of the water feature, raised pools offer the added benefit of providing seating if the walls are 13 inches to 16 inches high and the capstone is at least 1 foot wide.

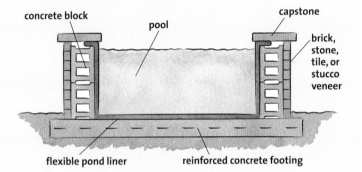

concrete block   pool   capstone

brick, stone, tile, or stucco veneer

flexible pond liner   reinforced concrete footing

▲ NO SPACE IS WASTED on this tiny patio. A single spout of water shoots high into the air, drawing attention to the low pool even from inside the house. Dense plantings cover the walls and surround the pool, softening the effect of all the hard surfaces and rectangular elements.

◄ THIS COZY GARDEN PATIO is truly a getaway since "floating" stepping-stones provide the path to get there. Solid, mortared piers beneath the stones ensure that the crossing will be safe.

► THIS LILY POOL was placed on axis with a pergola as a central focal point in a formal garden. Because the pool is only 1 foot deep, the water lily containers were placed directly on the bottom of the pool rather than staged on bricks or other supports.

Creating Ambience with Underwater Lighting

LIGHTING PLACED IN A POOL can create many different effects than lighting around a pool. One or more spotlights can be anchored on the bottom and aimed to highlight a fountain; floodlights can be built into the wall to illuminate the water in the pool; and fiber-optic lights can be mounted around the rim just beneath the coping for a mysterious glow. Keep in mind that water and electricity are a dangerous combination, so use only fixtures specially designed for underwater situations and hire an electrician to ensure that they are installed according to code.

◄ THE SINGLE UNDER-WATER SPOTLIGHT in this raised pool draws attention to the fountain. The round spheres provide a playful contrast to the strong linear aspects of the pool.

► FLAGSTONE PAVING extends slightly over the water to create a crisp edge on this geometric pool. The fountain spray head and dwarf papyrus, by contrast, share a free-spirited, upright habit that breaks the smooth plane of the still water to create a striking display.

▼ THE MINIMALIST DESIGN of this sunken pool, with its broad, cut-stone slabs for edging and paving, geometric design, neutral colors, and single water lily helps to create a calm, serene setting in this courtyard garden.

Wall Fountains

WALL FOUNTAINS, SHEET WATERFALLS, AND SPOUTS turn ordinary walls into focal points. They put the water near eye level, so they tend to be show-stoppers and, at times, even double as sculpture in the landscape. Because the water falls from a height, sound is one of a wall fountain's most appealing features, and when placed close to the house and within earshot of a bedroom, porch, kitchen, or other living area, the melody of the water can be enjoyed both inside and out.

Though courtyards are the quintessential spot for a wall fountain of any kind, with a little ingenuity, just about any wall can be enhanced with a wall fountain—whether a house wall, freestanding wall, or retaining wall. Even the wall of a pool or spa can be transformed into an exciting cascade or vanishing edge. The key is planning ahead, as plumbing is generally built into a cavity in the wall itself as the pool is being constructed.

▲ ▼ THIS SMALL PATIO with integrated raised pool is positioned slightly away from the house, creating a special backyard destination. The curving seat wall gets visitors up close to the whimsical frog fountains (the return pipes are hidden within the wall itself).

▲ THIS WALL FOUNTAIN AND POOL was inspired by the blue and white tiles the home-owners found on a trip to Spain. The Mediterranean-style fountain and tile paving suit both the home's architecture and the northern California climate.

▲ THIS CASCADING SHEET WATERFALL in an adobe wall anchors a small Santa Fe front-yard courtyard. Designed as a disappearing fountain, the water vanishes into a basin hidden beneath the river cobbles. The broad, flat wall provides an unobtrusive backdrop to the streaming water, rough boulders, smooth cobbles, and textured grasses.

NUTS AND BOLTS

Structural Wall Fountain

The best designed structural wall fountain will have the plumbing concealed within the wall itself. This requires a wall with an inner cavity or the drilling of one. Otherwise, the plumbing must run up the back of the wall, which is only an option if the back of the wall is not exposed to view. In most cases, the basin is probably large enough to contain the submersible pump and ample water, but if not, a separate sump basin can be constructed beneath the decorative basin. If the latter method is used, then a removable stone slab will be needed to allow access for maintenance. A wide range of spouts, rosettes, and decorative fountainheads can be built into a wall to complete the design.

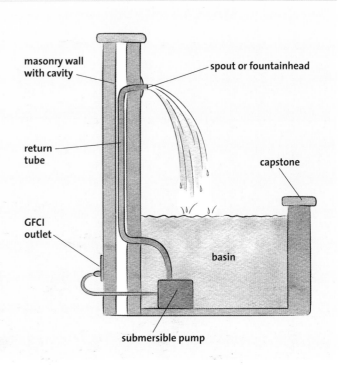

masonry wall with cavity

spout or fountainhead

return tube

capstone

GFCI outlet

basin

submersible pump

▼ ► ASIAN TRAVELS INSPIRED this one-of-a-kind fountain. It serves as the centerpiece of a lush garden retreat sandwiched in the narrow space between two large houses in downtown Oakland, California, and helps to mask the sound of the city's rail system, which passes through the same block.

▲ THIS FOUNTAIN, with its crumbling seat wall, looks like it was built long ago but in reality, it was discovered on display in an art gallery. The owners found a perfect home for it in the garden beneath a weeping mayten tree.

◄ THE SINUOUS CURVE of multiple copper spray heads may catch the eye, but the way the water bounces off the wall will hold your attention. The pattern is created because bricks were laid so that some protrude from the wall at different distances.

◀ SIMPLE, RUSTIC MATERIALS, like these field stones and roof tiles, can be used to create water features that stand the test of time. The umbrella-like foliage of lotus is easily contained between the wall and pool edge.

▼ THE PATIO, STONE WALL, AND FISH POND were carefully crafted in a naturalistic style so that they blend into the woodland garden. A small, spouting fountain placed in the water provides a subtle sound and aeration for the fish in hot weather (that's when the water holds the least amount of oxygen, but when the fish need it the most).

Sunken Concrete Pools

Concrete pools—which are essentially like small swimming pools and should be constructed by a professional—are both more expensive and more difficult to construct than lined ponds, but are considerably more permanent and durable. They are often the only logical choice for blending a pool with existing architecture. Concrete pools require reinforcement to prevent cracking in cold weather and should be carefully waterproofed. Their interiors may be painted various colors or they may be finished in sprayed-on pebble surfaces.

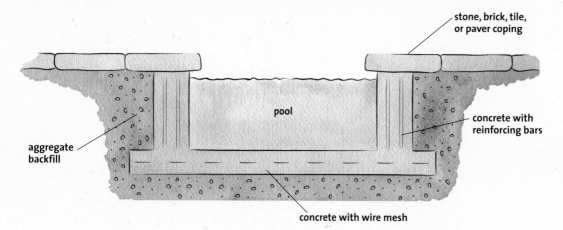

stone, brick, tile, or paver coping

pool

concrete with reinforcing bars

aggregate backfill

concrete with wire mesh

◄ THIS SCULPTED COPPER wall fountain
was designed by a landscape architect—
not as a hanging wall fountain, but as an
integrated part of the retaining wall with
embedded return pipes, concealed control
valves, and a sunken pool.

▲ STONE IS AN EXCELLENT transitional material since it
relates to a home and yet as a natural material, it visually connects to the landscape beyond. This makes it a good choice for
a landscape feature that isn't tied directly to the house like this
half-circle pond and retaining wall.

▲ THIS CHISELED GRANITE FOUNTAIN features
two small pools of water connected by a cascade.
The ledge protrudes slightly so that water falls
directly into the bottom pool rather than trickling
down the side of the stone. It makes for a warm welcome, since it's located near the front door.

◄ WALL FOUNTAINS, moss-covered brick, and ivy
are synonymous with the shaded courtyard gardens
of the Old South. Rubbing a bit of buttermilk on
brick will help speed up the growth of moss on a
new fountain to give it an ages-old look.

▲ STRONG CONTRASTS make this water feature striking: black stone against a white wall; dark water recessed below a light-colored patio; the rippled surface of the stone adjacent to the still water of the basin. Water sparkles in sunlight as it cascades over the dark stone.

► THIS CRESCENT-SHAPED POOL serves as an extension of the patio. The style of stone construction changes from cut stone to stacked field stone as it moves away from the house and patio, making a gradual transition from architectural to natural spaces in the landscape.

▲ WATER, LIKE SOIL, is a wonderful planting medium. The tile-edged pool beneath this wall fountain is filled with water-loving plants of all shapes, sizes, and textures. The plants also create shade and hiding places desired by the goldfish that make their home in the pool.

► SCULPTURE CAN BE functional as well as beautiful. This water wall and wavy bench, which is positioned along a wall in a small entry courtyard, is a perfect example. Water trickling irregularly over the sculpted wall is accented by three uplights after dusk.

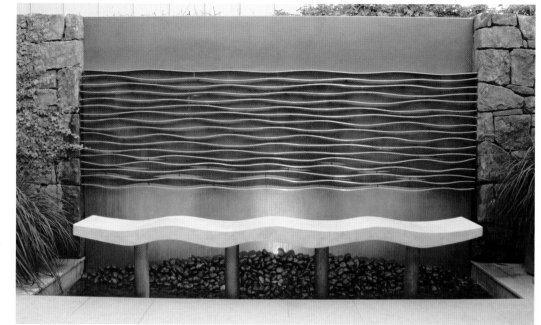

▲ ON SLOPED LOTS, WATER GARDENS CAN EXTEND out from the bottom of a retaining wall or, as in this case, be built behind the retaining wall. A narrow planting pocket was created along the edge of this pool to soften the hard surfaces of the stone.

► THE COZY PATIO created just outside this home's finished basement includes a small pool built into the retaining wall of the sunken garden. Both the retaining walls and pavers were dry laid, with small pockets left for creeping and trailing plants, enhancing the casual nature of this getaway spot.

Submerged Plants

Also called "oxygenators," these underwater plants produce the oxygen that fish and tadpoles need to survive. They also help filter the water by removing fish wastes and mineral salts. Plan on growing one bunch of oxygenators for each 1 to 2 square feet of water surface. The bunches can either be weighted to the bottom with a rock, or planted in sand or gravel.

Anacharis	(*Egeria densa*)
Canadian pondweed	(*Elodea canadensis*)
Eel grass	(*Vallisneria americana*)
Fanwort	(*Cabomba caroliniana*)
Hairgrass	(*Eleocharis acicularis*)
Hornwort	(*Ceratophyllum demersum*)
Parrot's feather	(*Myriophyllum aquaticum*)*
Pondweed	(*Potamogeton* spp.)
Water hyssop	(*Bacopa caroliniana*)

*Considered invasive or banned in AL, CT, ME, MA, VT, and WA. Never release any water garden plants into natural waterways in any state.

▲ THE FEATHERY FOLIAGE OF PARROT'S FEATHER makes it a popular submerged plant for water gardens. However, it has been banned from several states for its invasive tendencies; if your state still allows it, grow it with caution and never release it into natural waterways.

▲ THIS WALL FOUNTAIN SPILLS into a rectangular pool that must be crossed in order to reach the upper garden. It is an ingenious design for a very steep, shallow San Francisco backyard that could only be made accessible through terracing.

◄ IT TAKES A SKILLED STONEMASON to craft the unusual concave walls that give this pool a grotto-like ambience. The fountain creates a dominant focal point in a corner of the landscape where plantings are kept simple.

▼ MATCHING WALL FOUNTAINS with spigot spouts provide double the pleasure in this pea-gravel courtyard, where the emphasis is on architecture and water. Plantings play a secondary role, as ivy frames the fountains with a wall of greenery.

▼ PEBBLE-MOSAIC STRUCTURES like this raised pool and spouting wall are not difficult to build, but they require considerable patience and a creative eye. This goldfish pond was built at sitting height in the front yard of a neighborhood where everyone enjoys visiting while taking evening walks.

▲ TERRACED PROPERTIES OFFER UNIQUE OPPORTUNITIES to create water features. A channel of recirculating water runs across an upper terrace, cascading over this stone retaining wall into a rectangular pool below. The round river cobbles in the cascade contrast with the quarried stone in the wall.

◀ ALTHOUGH THE RETAINING WALL defines the entry courtyard for this home, the fountain makes it a welcoming space. By using the same stone in the house, fountain, and retaining walls, the outdoor room feels like a natural extension of the house.

▼ THIS RECTANGULAR FISH POND was built next to a patio and pergola in a courtyard garden. The garden is densely planted, with ferns and vines allowed to fall loosely over the edges of the pool. This creates a relaxed environment where the owners can spend time with their grandchildren and friends.

▲ THIS WALL FOUNTAIN FEATURES a built-in spout but a freestanding concrete basin—an innovative way to use decorative statuary containers, as well as oversized copper tubs and other antique or collectible basins.

▲ THE COVERED PAVILION feels like it should be on a small island, especially since it requires crossing the water on "floating" stone steps to get there. Both the pool and sitting area, while beautiful during the day, take on a glow when the sun sets and the subtle landscape lighting is turned on.

CASCADES

▼ DISTINCTIVE, ROUNDED COBBLES were used in this tiered water feature, the terrace retaining wall, and the fireplace hearth to create a sense of unity throughout the outdoor living areas. The cobbles are of considerable heft, which helps put the walls and pools in scale with the house.

Building Codes and Regulations

MANY WATER FEATURES—especially those over 2 feet deep or that are permanently constructed—fall under the jurisdiction of local building codes. Rules and regulations regarding the size, depth, location, setback requirements, permits, and construction methods vary considerably from one town to another and could have considerable impact on your design. Electrical codes apply to water features with recirculating pumps or submersible lighting. Ponds or pools over a certain depth (often as little as 24 inches) may require fencing or other safety measures. In addition to checking building codes, make sure all underground utilities have been clearly marked before any digging begins.

▲ THE EMPHASIS IN THIS GARDEN is on pattern. The two square pools are the same shape and size as the checkerboard paving and grass squares on the lower terrace. The cascade runs through a narrow channel before spilling into the lower pond.

◄ CASCADES CAN BE EITHER separate elements built into a wall or an integral part of the wall itself, as shown here. The same stone used to build the wall was used to create this cascade that allows water to fall gently into the pool below.

▲ ANTIQUES AND FLEA MARKET FINDS, like this hand pump, can be put to good use as fountains. This one readily brings to mind a watering well.

▲ NOT ONE, BUT THREE WEEPING CASCADES make this wall an intriguing element in the landscape. Asymmetric placement of the cascades creates a balanced design. Similarly, the weeping wall dominates only one-third of the circular pool edge, visually balancing the remaining lighter coping.

▶ WHEN DESIGNING WATER FEATURES with multiple elements, it's helpful to think in terms of sources, courses, and destinations. This raised pool is a source. The cascade and rill are both watercourses. A sunken pool, from which the water is recirculated, is the destination.

SWIMMING POOL FEATURES

▼ ▶ THIS POOL WAS DESIGNED WITH A REVERSE INFINITY EDGE—one that falls toward the house rather than toward the distant landscape—allowing the homeowner to view the cascade from indoors. In another unique twist, the water trickles irregularly over the stacked stone wall before vanishing beneath pebbles into a hidden recirculation reservoir rather than splashing into an exposed basin. The spa also overflows into an underground reservoir for recirculation.

► NATURALISTIC IN DESIGN, this large waterfall was built into the pool's edge and surrounded by bold plantings. It spills over in several places, creating pockets where swimmers can stand beneath the falling water.

Sheet Waterfalls

Sheet waterfalls are those flat "sheets" of water that spill out of a wall rather than over it. While it appears that water is flowing through a narrow slot, it is actually being forced through a series of small holes by a recirculating pump. Sheet waterfalls are made from brass, copper, or stainless steel and sold as a unit that is installed inside the wall and connected to a submersible pump in the basin via plumbing.

◄ ▲ A SHEET WATERFALL was built into a stacked-stone retaining wall above this swimming pool. It was placed on axis with the house so that it could be viewed from the living room, which has French doors opening onto the pool deck.

▲ THE STONE RETAINING WALL on the upper side of this pool camouflages a spa that was built into the hillside. Water cascades from the spa into the pool over a single rock ledge that extends several inches beyond the wall to allow the water to fall directly into the basin rather than to trickle down the rocks.

▶ THIS EXPANSIVE OUTDOOR ROOM was designed for entertaining. The cascade from the spa to the pool provides not only a visual focal point but also the sweet sound of falling water that soothes guests.

▲ LARGE ROUND PLANTERS
that echo the design of a raised
spa anchor two corners of this
pool. Water flows through a slot
just below the capstone, creating a spa-like cascade. The pool
also has a vanishing-edge water
feature along one side connecting
the two planters.

▶ THIS COMBINATION
waterfall-cascade makes
a big splash into a swimming
pool. Even so, it doesn't overwhelm the backyard with sound
because the setting is a broad,
open southwestern landscape
where sound tends to get lost.

Watercourses

WATERCOURSES GO BY MANY NAMES: channels, rills, runnels, or canals. Those that tumble down steps are commonly called water stairs. Most are filled with flowing water, but moatlike canals with still or barely moving water can also be intriguing. Long, narrow watercourses are ideal for visually connecting different spaces or even different levels within a landscape. And when their bends disappear around shrubs or garden structures, they create a sense of adventure.

Like streams, most architectural watercourses have both a source and an outlet—usually a fountain on one end and a pool on the other. However, they differ from streams in their shape, style, and construction materials. Even if natural materials such as stone are used to create watercourses, they are often used in highly stylized ways. Architectural watercourses have clean lines—whether straight, zigzagging, or serpentine. They can be constructed below ground, above ground, or even cascading down a staircase.

◄ THIS WATERCOURSE PHYSICALLY AND VISUALLY connects a divided, split-level backyard, thus encouraging the use of all areas. It's hard not to feel compelled to follow the water as it travels across a patio, tumbles down steps, flows through a canal, and spills into a fish pond.

◄ ▼ WATER WENDS ITS WAY DOWN the length of a narrow, sloped side yard, moving through a series of small ponds, fountains, and channels along the way. It was constructed mostly from recycled materials and is surrounded by a densely planted and colorful garden.

▲ THIS SEVERAL-FOOT-WIDE, dark-bottomed canal divides a densely planted garden into distinct sections that are easily accessed by a simply designed and sturdily constructed wooden bridge. The dark bottom makes the canal appear deeper than it really is.

▶ THIS 18-INCH-DEEP, irregularly shaped canal surrounds a backyard dining area like a moat surrounds a castle, defining its boundaries as an outdoor room even though it doesn't have any walls. The moat also serves as a home to goldfish.

◄ THE WIDE PATIO STEPS allow for seating to enjoy the watercourse that spills from a raised pool and tumbles down the steps through a narrow channel. Herb-filled planting pockets placed near the fountain and along the steps lend a sense of lushness to the setting.

NUTS AND BOLTS

Floating Steps

Stepping-stones that appear to "float" in the water are an excellent alternative to bridges in shallow water. Visually, they are both less intrusive and more intriguing. To keep them from becoming slippery, they should only be used in still or slow moving water that is no more than a foot deep, and they should rise at least an inch or two above the maximum water level.

Select very thick stones that won't crack when stepped on or during a winter freeze, and make sure they have a flat, relatively level surface. A bit of rough texture (versus a smooth, slick stone) will provide better traction. Concrete pavers or artificial stones may also be used.

Construction of floating steps is fairly straightforward: The stones are set with mortar on broad piers of brick or concrete that extend almost to the edges of the stepping stones. These piers, in turn, are set atop concrete footings for stability. If a pond liner is used, the footings should be built before the liner is laid and two layers of thick underlayment should be used to protect the liner from the pier.

▲ THESE FLOATING BLUESTONE STEPS zigzag through a garden filled with multiple water features. Though the water is contained in a narrow channel just beneath the steps, the surrounding water features give the impression that this is part of a much larger body of water.

thick stepping stone

mortared brick

underlayment

pond liner

concrete footing

Resources

ADDITIONAL READING

Aquascape Lifestyles magazine. www.nawgs.com/lifestylesmagazine

Complete Guide to Water Gardens, by Kathleen Fisher. Creative Homeowner Press, 2000.

Creating Water Gardens, by Denny Schrock. Ortho Books, 2003.

Designing Water Gardens: A Unique Approach, by Anthony Archer-Wills. Conran, distributed by Sterling, 2000.

Gardening with Water: How James van Sweden and Wolfgang Oehme Built and Plant Fountains, Swimming Pools, Lily Pools, Ponds and Water Edges, by James van Sweden. Random House, 1995 (first edition).

The Master Book of the Water Garden: The Ultimate Guide to the Design and Maintenance of the Water Garden, by Phillip Swindells. Bulfinch, 2002.

Ortho's All About Garden Pools and Fountains, by Veronica Larson Fowler. Ortho Books, 1999.

Quick and Easy Container Water Gardens, by Philip Swindells. Storey Books, 1998.

SOMA Basics Water Features, by David Stevens. SOMA Basics, rev. ed. of a Conran Octopus book, 2000.

Water Features for Small Gardens: From Concept to Construction, by Keith Davitt. Timber Press, 2003.

The Water Gardener: A Complete Guide to Designing, Constructing and Planting Water Features, by Anthony Archer-Wills. Todtri productions, 2002.

Water Gardening: The Magazine for Pondkeepers www.watergardening.com

Water Gardens, by Susan Lang & T. Jeff Williams. Sunset Books, 2004.

Water Gardens: Simple Projects, Contemporary Designs, by Hazel White. Chronicle Books 1998.

FOUNTAINS AND WATER GARDENING SUPPLIES

Atlanta Water Gardens
www.atlantawatergardens.com

Blue Water Fountains & Garden Gallery
www.bluewaterfountains.com

Fountains Unique
www.fountainsunique.com

LaSorgente Glass Studio
www.nightorbs.com

Maine Millstones
www.mainemillstones.com

North Bay Ponds & Water
www.nbponds.com

Range West
www.rangewest.com

Smith & Hawken
www.smithandhawken.com

Stone Forest
www.stoneforest.com

Wakoola Water Gardens
www.wakoola.com

The Water Garden
www.watergarden.com

Yoshikawa
www.yoshistone.com

SPECIALTY NURSERIES

Aquatic Plant Depot
www.aquaticplantdepot.com

Arizona Aquatic Gardens
www.azgardens.com

Lilypons Water Gardens
www.lilypons.com

Tropical Pond & Garden
www.tropicalpond.com

William Tricker, Inc.
www.tricker.com

DESIGNERS SPECIALIZING IN WATER FEATURES

Allgood Outdoors
www.allgoodoutdoors.com

Aquascape Designs
www.aquascapedesigns.com

Aquatic Construction
www.aquaticconstruction.com

Backyard Watergardens, LLC
www.backyardwatergardens.com

The Fockele Garden Company
www.fockelegardencompany.com

Potomac Waterworks
www.potomacwaterworks.com

Rik Rock Architectural Water Environments
www.rikrock.com

ORGANIZATIONS

Associated Koi Clubs of America
www.akca.org

Certified Aquascape Contractors
www.certifiedaquascapecontractor.com

International Professional Pond Contractors Association
www.ippca.com

International Waterlily & Water Gardening Society
www.iwgs.org

National Association of Pond Professionals
www.nationalpondpro.com

North American Water Garden Society
www.nawgs.com

Water Gardeners International
www.watergardenersinternational.org

Credits

Chapter 1

p. 5: Photo © Lee Anne White; design: Margaret Mosely

p. 6: (top right) Photo © Lee Anne White; design: Keith Geller; (bottom right and left) Photo © Jerry Pavia

p. 7: Photo © Allan Mandell; design: George Little and David Lewis

p.8: (left)Photo © Lee Anne White; design: Carrie Nimmer; (right) Photo © Lee Anne White; design: Naomi Sachs; garden: Robert McLaughlin

p.9: (top left) Photo © Allan Mandell; design: Rick Serazin; (top right) Photo © Lee Anne White; design: George Little and David Lewis; (bottom) Photo © Lee Anne White; design: Lee Anne White

p. 10: Photo © Lee Anne White; design Ann Nichols

p. 11: Photo (top) © Lee Anne White; design: Paul and Robin Cowley, Potomac Waterworks; (bottom) Photo © Brian Vanden Brink; design: Horiuchi & Solien Landscape Architects

p. 12: (top) Photo © Lee Anne White; design: Ryan Gainey; (bottom) © Allan Mandell; design: Tom Chakas and Roger Raiche

p. 13 Photo © Lee Anne White; design: Paul and Robin Cowley, Potomac Waterworks

p. 14: (top) Photo © Deidra Walpole; design: Bea Grow; (bottom) Photo © Deidra Walpole

p. 15: (top) Photo © Lee Anne White; design: Joan Lewis; (bottom) Photo © Jerry Pavia

p. 16: (top) Photo © Lee Anne White; design: Eve Thyrum; (bottom) Photo © Lee Anne White; design: George Little and David Lewis

p. 17: Photos © Lee Anne White

p. 18: (top) Photo © Lee Anne White; artist: Jane Kelly; (bottom left) Photo © Lee Anne White; design: Jeni Webber; (bottom right) Photo © J. Paul Moore

p. 19: (top) Photo © J. Paul Moore; (bottom) Photo © Lee Anne White; design: Jeni Webber

p. 20: (top) Photo Steve Silk; © The Taunton Press, Inc.; design: Joseph Tomocik; (bottom) Photo © Rich Pomerantz; design: Conway Nursery

p. 21: Photo Steve Silk; © The Taunton Press, Inc.; design: Joseph Tomocik

p. 22: (top) Photo © Lee Anne White; design: McKee Botanical Garden; (bottom) Photo © Allan Mandell; design: Elizabeth Lair

p. 23: (top) Photo © Lee Anne White; design: Lee Anne White; (bottom) Photo © Mark Turner

p. 24: (top) Photo © Lee Anne White; design: Four Dimensions; garden: Gail Giffen; (bottom) Photo © Allan Mandell; design: Tom Chakas and Roger Raiche

p. 25: Photo © Allan Mandell; design: George Little and David Lewis

CHAPTER 2

p. 27: Photo © Lee Anne White; design: Dan Cleveland

p. 28: (right) Photo © Dency Kane; design: Martin Viette Nurseries; (left) Photo © Mark Turner

p. 29: Photo © Lee Anne White; design: Mark and Mildred Fockele

p. 30: Photo © Dency Kane

p. 31: (top) Photo © Lee Anne White; (bottom) Photo © Lee Anne White; design: Paula Refi; garden: Barbara & Gordon Robinson

p. 32: Photo © Lee Anne White; residence: Carl and Jennifer Romberg

p. 33: (top) Photo © Jerry Pavia; (bottom) Photo © Lee Anne White; design: Ann Nichols

p. 34: Photo © Lee Anne White; design: Ben G. Page, Jr; garden: Mrs. Walter M. Robinson, Jr.

p. 35 (top) Photo © Mark Turner; (bottom) Photo © Lee Anne White; design: Wakoola Water Gardens

p. 36: Photo © Lee Anne White; design: Wakoola Water Gardens

p. 37: (left) Photo © Lee Anne White; design: F. Malcom George; (right) Photo © Lee Anne White; design: Michelle Derviss

p. 38: Photo © Deidra Walpole; design: Karen Dominguez-Brann

p. 39: Photos © Lee Anne White; design: George Little and David Lewis

p. 40: (top) Photo © Lee Anne White; design: The Fockele Garden Company; garden: Larry and Dee North; (bottom) Photo © Lee Anne White; design: George Little and David Lewis

p. 41: Photos © Lee Anne White; design: Jeni Webber

p. 42: Photos © Lee Anne White; design: The Fockele Garden Company, Chris Condon, & Andrew Crawford

p. 43: (left) Photo © Lee Anne White; garden: Betty Romberg; (right) Photo © Lee Anne White; design: Wakoola Water Gardens

p. 44: Photo: Lee Anne White; artist: Barton Rubenstein

p. 45: (left) Photo © Lee Anne White; design: Stone Forest, Inc.; (right) Photo © Lee Anne White

p. 46: (top left) Photo © Lee Anne White; design: The Fockele Garden Company; garden: Scotty Pannell; (top right) Photo © Lee Anne White; design: P.O.P.S. Landscaping; (bottom) Photo © Lee Anne White; design: Rochelle Ford

p. 47: Photo © Lee Anne White; design: The Fockele Garden Company; garden: Scotty Pannell

p. 48: Photo © Carolyn L. Bates; design: Colleen Steen

p. 49: (top left) Photo © Lee Anne White; design: Four Dimensions; garden: Gail Giffen; (top right) Photo © Dency Kane; (bottom) Photo © Deidra Walpole

p. 50: Photo © Jerry Pavia

p. 51: (top) Photo © Lee Anne White; design: George Little and David Lewis; (bottom) Photo © Lee Anne White; design: Joan Lewis

p. 52: (top) Photo © Deidra Walpole; design: New Leaf Landscape Design; (bottom) Photo © Lee Anne White; design: Jeni Webber

p. 53: (top) Photo © Lee Anne White; design: Richard McPherson; garden: San Tran; (bottom) Photo © Lee Anne White; lighting design: Anna Kondolf

p. 54: (left) Photo © Allan Mandell; design: Zen Gardens, Yoshihiro Kawasaki; (right) © Allan Mandell; Portland International Gardens

p. 55: Photo © Allan Mandell; design: Venita Aldrich and Jerry Barswess

p. 56: (top) Photo © Brian Vanden Brink; design: Horiuchi and Solien Landscape Architects; (left) Photo © Mark Turner

p. 57: Photo © Lee Anne White; design: Cheekwood Botanical Garden

p. 58: (top) Photo © Lee Anne White; design: Luis Llenza; garden: Bruce Borger; (bottom) Photo © Lee Anne White; design: David McMullin

p. 59: Photo © Lee Anne White; design: Clemens and Associates

p. 60: (top) Photo © Lee Anne White; design: Joan Lewis; (bottom) Photo © Lee Anne White; design: Stone Forest, Inc.

p. 61: (left) Photo © Lee Anne White; design: Paul & Robin Cowley, Potomac Waterworks; (right) Photo © Lee Anne White; design: Wakoola Water Gardens

p. 62 (top) Photo © Lee Anne White; design: Four Dimensions; artist: Mavis McClure; garden: Gail Giffen; (left) Photo © Lee Anne White; design: Sydney Eddison; artists: Elizabeth McDonald & Trevor Youngberg; (bottom) Photo © Lee Anne White; design: The Fockele Garden Company; garden: Robin and Tricia Terrell

p. 63: Photos © Lee Anne White; design: Naomi Sachs

p. 64: (top) Photo © Lee Anne White; design: The Fockele Garden Company; (bottom) Photo © Lee Anne White; design: Stone Forest, Inc.

p. 65: Photos © Lee Anne White; design: David Ellis, Ellis LanDesign

p. 66: (top left) Photo © Lee Anne White; design: Joshua Gannon, RangeWest Gallery; (bottom left) Photo © Lee Anne White; design: The Fockele Garden Company; (right) Photo © Lee Anne White; design: Stone Forest, Inc.

p. 67: (top) Photo Lee Anne White; design: Clemens and Associates; garden: David and Peggy Ater; (bottom) Photo © Lee Anne White; design: Wakoola Water Gardens

p. 68: (top) Photo © Lee Anne White; design: Four Dimensions; (bottom) Photo © Lee Anne White; design: P.O.P.S. Landscaping

p. 69: Photos © Lee Anne White; design: Hermann Weis

p. 70: (top) Photo © Lee Anne White; design: Mark and Beverly Williams; (bottom) Photo © Lee Anne White; design: Wakoola Water Gardens

p. 71: (top and bottom right) Photos © Lee Anne White; design: Wakoola Water Gardens; (bottom left) Photo © Lee Anne White; design: Stone Forest, Inc.

p. 72: Photos © Lee Anne White; design: Stone Forest, Inc.

p. 73: (top and bottom left) Photos © Lee Anne White; design: Stone Forest, Inc.; (right) Photo © Lee Anne White

CHAPTER 3

p. 74: Photo © Lee Anne White; design: Wakoola Water Gardens

p. 76: (top) Photo © J. Paul Moore; (bottom) Photo © Lee Anne White; design: Karin & Larry Guzy

p. 77: (left) Photo © Allan Mandell; design: Matt Sander Landscaping; (right) Photo © Lee Anne White; design: The Fockele Garden Company

p. 78: (top left and right) Photos © Brian Vanden Brink; (bottom) Photo © Lee Anne White; design: William Hewitt

p. 79: (top) Photo © Lee Anne White; design: Luiz Llenza; (bottom) Photo © Lee Anne White; design: Karin & Larry Guzy

pp. 80–81: Photos © Lee Anne White; design: Paul & Robin Cowley, Potomac Waterworks

p. 82: (top) Photo © Carolyn L. Bates; landscape design: The Cushman Design Group; pond construction: Sundown Corporation; (bottom) Photo © Lee Anne White; design: Jon Carloftis

p. 83: (top left) Photo © Lee Anne White; design: David Ellis, Ellis LanDesign; (bottom left) Photo © Lee Anne White; design: The Fockele Garden Company; (bottom right) Photo © Lee Anne White

p. 84: (left) Photo © Allan Mandell; design: Jeff Glander; (right) Photo © Jerry Pavia

p. 85: (top) Photo © Lee Anne White; design: The Fockele Garden Company; (middle) Photo © Mark Turner; (bottom) Photo © Lee Anne White; design: Stephen Carruthers

p. 86: Photo © Jerry Pavia

p. 87: (top left) Photo © Deidra Walpole; (top right) Photo © Lee Anne White; design: Randall Tate, The Water Garden; (bottom) Photo © Mark Turner

p. 88: (top) Photo © Lee Anne White; design: Randall Tate, The Water Garden; (bottom) Photo © Lee Anne White; design: Clemens and Associates; residence: Wilson and Jenna Scanlan

p. 89: Photo © J. Paul Moore

p. 90: (top) Photo © Lee Anne White; design: Wakoola Water Gardens; (bottom) Photo © Lee Anne White; design: The Fockele Garden Company

p. 91: Photo © Lee Anne White; design: Jeni Webber

p. 92: (left) Photo © Jerry Pavia; (top right) Photo © Lee Anne White; design: Randall Tate, The Water Garden; (bottom right) Photo © Lee Anne White; design: Karin & Larry Guzy

p. 93: (top) Photos © Lee Anne White; design: Hermann Weis; installation: The Fockele Garden Company

p. 94: (top) Photo © Lee Anne White; design: Mel Berss; (bottom) Photo © Lee Anne White; design: The Fockele Garden Company

p. 95: (top left) Photo © Lee Anne White; (bottom left) Photo © Lee Anne White; design: The Fockele Garden Company; (bottom right) Photo © Alan & Linda Detrick

p. 96: (left) Photo © Lee Anne White; design: Enchantment Custom Builders; (right) Photo © Mark Turner; design: Bellevue Botanic Garden

p. 97: (top) Photo © Alan & Linda Detrick; (bottom) Photo © Lee Anne White; design: Simmonds & Associates; construction: Four Dimensions

p. 98: Photos © Jerry Pavia

p. 99: (left) Photo © Deidra Walpole; design: California Waterscapes; (right) Photo © Mark Turner

p. 100: (left) Photo © Lee Anne White; design: The Fockele Garden Company; (right) Photo © Lee Anne White; design: Longue Vue Gardens

p. 101: (top) Photo © Lee Anne White; design: Wakoola Water Gardens; (bottom) Photo © J. Paul Moore

p. 102: (left) Photo © Lee Anne White; design: Four Dimensions; garden: Kern and Arlene Hildebrand; (top right) Photo © Lee Anne White; design: Stone Forest, Inc.; (bottom right) Photo © Lee Anne White; design: Four Dimensions; garden: Joe McClintock

p. 103: Photo © Lee Anne White; design: Richmond Hill Inn

p. 104: (left) Photo © Lee Anne White; design: Scott Arboretum; (right) Photo © Lee Anne White; design: P.O.P.S. Landscaping

p. 105: (top left and bottom) Photos © Lee Anne White; design: Paula Refi; stonework: Clemons & Rice; residence: Barbara and Gordon Robinson; (top right) Photo © Lee Anne White; design: Hermann Weis

p. 106: Photo © Lee Anne White; design: Derviss + Chavis Design + Build; residence: Jeff and Carole Dandridge

p. 107: (top left and top right) Photos © Lee Anne White; design: The Fockele Garden Company; (bottom) Photo © Lee Anne White; design: David & Michelle Gordon, Desert Sage Builders

p. 108: (top) Photo © Allan Mandell; (bottom) Photo © Jerry Pavia

p. 109: (top) Photo © Lee Anne White; design: P.O.P.S. Landscaping; residence: Larry and Debbie Niffin; (bottom) Photo © Deidra Walpole

p. 110: Photos © Jerry Pavia

p. 111: Photo © Dency Kane

p. 112: (top) Photo © Alan & Linda Detrick; design: Wave Hill; (bottom) Photo © Alan & Linda Detrick; design: Marilyn Coombe Stewart

p. 113: (top) Photo © Dency Kane; garden: Valerie Strong; (bottom) Photo © Lee Anne White; design: Paul & Robin Cowley, Potomac Waterworks

p. 114: (top) Photo © Lee Anne White; (bottom) Photo © Alan & Linda Detrick

p. 115: (top) Photo © Allan Mandell; design: Jan Hopkins; (bottom) Photo © Allan Mandell

For More Great Design Ideas, Look for These and Other Taunton Press Books Wherever Books are Sold.

NEW KITCHEN IDEA BOOK
1-56158-693-5
Product #070773
$19.95 U.S./$27.95 Canada

NEW BATHROOM IDEA BOOK
1-56158-692-7
Product #070774
$19.95 U.S./$27.95 Canada

NEW KIDSPACE IDEA BOOK
1-56158-694-3
Product #070776
$19.95 U.S./$27.95 Canada

NEW BUILT-INS IDEA BOOK
1-56158-673-0
Product #070755
$19.95 U.S./$27.95 Canada

TRIM IDEA BOOK
1-56158-710-9
Product #070786
$19.95 U.S./$27.95 Canada

TILE IDEA BOOK
1-56158-709-5
Product #070785
$19.95 U.S./$27.95 Canada

STONESCAPING IDEA BOOK
1-56158-763-X
Product #070824
$14.95 U.S./$21.00 Canada

OUTDOOR LIVING IDEA BOOK
1-56158-757-5
Product #070820
$19.95 U.S./$27.95 Canada

ORGANIZING IDEA BOOK
1-56158-780-X
Product #070835
$14.95 U.S./$21.00 Canada

CURB APPEAL IDEA BOOK
1-56158-803-2
Product #070853
$19.95 U.S./$27.95 Canada

TAUNTON'S HOME STORAGE IDEA BOOK
1-56158-676-5
Product #070758
$19.95 U.S./$27.95 Canada

TAUNTON'S FAMILY HOME IDEA BOOK
1-56158-729-X
Product #070789
$19.95 U.S./$27.95 Canada

TAUNTON'S HOME WORKSPACE IDEA BOOK
ISBN 1-56158-701-X
Product #070783
$19.95 U.S./$27.95 Canada

BACKYARD IDEA BOOK
1-56158-667-6
Product #070749
$19.95 U.S./$27.95 Canada

POOL IDEA BOOK
1-56158-764-8
Product #070825
$19.95 U.S./$27.95 Canada

BABYSPACE IDEA BOOK
1-56158-799-0
Product #070857
$14.95 U.S./$21.00 Canada

DECORATING IDEA BOOK
1-56158-762-1
Product #070829
$24.95 U.S./$34.95 Canada

WINDOW TREATMENT IDEA BOOK
1-56158-819-9
Product #070869
$19.95 U.S./$26.95 Canada